CW00686802

THE A___
OF HAIKU
2000

A guide to haiku, senryu, tanka, haibun,
renga, sedoka, sijo and related genres.

edited by
Gerald England

published by
New Hope International

20 Werneth Avenue, Gee Cross, Hyde, Cheshire,
SK14 5NL,
UK

2000

Acknowledgments:
"A Moth for La Tour" by Linda Jeanette Ward first appeared in *Frogpond*. Helen Buckingham's haiku beginning "a scent ..." first appeared in *Still*. The haiku by Max Verhart first appeared in SOME BREATH (Private Press 't Hoge Woord).

Cover design by Jean M. Kahler

For *New Hope International* omnibus subscribers this *Special Edition Chapbook* forms Volume 21 ##1 & 2

British Library Cataloguing in Publication Data. A catalogue record for this book is available from the British Library.

A website supporting this publication is to be found at
http://www.crosswinds.net/ ~ werneth/hk.htm

ISBN 0 903610 24 8

INTRODUCTION

Many people get perplexed when they first encounter haiku. They are often told that it is a Japanese verse form consisting of 17 syllables written in three lines of 5-7-5. They may also be told about the requirement to include a season-word. On seeing published haiku that contain other than 17 syllables they become confused.

Before haiku there was renga, a regal and highly-regulated form of verse with Chinese antecedents. Modern haiku was born in 17th century Japan. It arose, not so much from a need to write poetry as to express the feelings of Zen. For many, haiku, is not just another way to package content. It is a way of life; an open-ness to and one-ness with nature. In Japan poetry and haiku are separate entities. There, people **do haiku**; writing haiku refers to calligraphy.

Those who have studied the form and become masters of it (haijin), will tell you that a haiku is essentially the distillation of a moment. Haiku are set in nature (in the widest possible sense) and they reflect the human response to nature. Often this is by the juxtaposition of images. Essential ingredients for haiku are simplicity of language, directness of communication, rhythm and the relative absence of the narrator. The trap into which poets new to haiku often fall is in using the techniques of other poetries inappropriately. Simile, alliteration, metaphor, rhyme, personification, intellectualisation and other such devices have little place in haiku. Also, since haiku are meant to be complete in themselves, a title is generally considered an unnecessary addition.

You will discover many poems published under the title "haiku" that do not observe these rules — many will have a genuine haiku quality and be perfectly admissible as haiku. Others might well be mis-named as haiku — but be quite acceptable under the label of "short poem". *The Haiku Society of America* spent six years in committees trying to come up with a definition satisfactory for use by dictionaries. Even now they are not completely happy with it.

The articles in this volume are intended to inform and instruct, but beyond that, readers will learn by studying the examples here. Above all though — enjoy them!

Gerald England

CONTENTS

Articles   Original writing   *Artwork*

4

MY HAIKU LOVE AFFAIR

Ah! The Haiku! Ambrosia of the gods! "A moment of exquisite awareness! ...A moment of exalted consciousness!" A Japanese haikuist said "If a man writes only one, real, good haiku in his lifetime, this should be par for the course!" It isn't too often we mortals are so blessed by grace as to experience the hallowness of heaven-sent haiku.

Children in elementary grades are taught to write haiku using the traditional 5-7-5 format of structured verse, but it takes a fully mature adult, who has been through the mill of life, to be capable of haiku. It was in my forties that the haiku crossed my path. I applied myself to mastering the form and wrote many.

The real blessing is what the haiku did for me as I continued the discipline of writing. It was a stepping-stone into other forms of expression. By dint of writing haiku, wrestling with clauses and phrases, so as to get my whole thought into seventeen syllables, I had to search for the exact word, embodying my meaning, to use that word to replace a whole phrase or clause. This took some doing, but I loved the challenge and by continuing in this manner got so that I developed and honed my writing talent so that a whole drama or meaningful diatribe for the newspapers could be written on a postcard, or even a calling card.

I have tried to eke from other haikuists whether or not they felt the same way. So far I haven't come across any person who could even faintly realize what I was driving at. They liked the haiku just as it was, it having no other reason for existence, but just to be written.

Do I stand alone in my great love for the haiku and what it has done for me and meant to me? Earth-bound in my dedication to various issues of mundane importance to humanity today, I write few haiku now. However, as I walked recently in our beautiful, north temperate rain forest park, the following haiku made itself felt.

> bleak, dark rainy day...
> sun-break...rhododendron leaves
> silver-dew sparkled.

Jessie Hraska

August morning —
watching me watch it,
the feral cat

In the chapel
the smell of stone
and wine must

Neca Stoller

a sparrow
fills the courtyard
Sunday afternoon

dripping slowly
down her perfect lower lip
banana cream pie

Marc Thompson

to find me
to find you
fading polaroid

sandcastle
mine
was here

body hair wearing moonlight

ai li

raaaainy Sunday —
fresh baked bread
cooling ...

partial eclipse —
she takes another
bite of biscuit

Sue Mill

Licked clean
only the worm pill left
in the cat's bowl.

in each red tomato —
a hole the size
of a chicken's beak.

Nona Welander

Seagull tracks
over wet sand ~
another wave

small boy
jump step step   jump step step
joints in footpath

John Bird

an old folks home;
residents doze slack-jawed
in the morning sun

October sunlight
brightens a corridor —
wheelchairs in a row

Francine Porad

nightswimming
across lonely waters
the clarity of your voice

at the roadside
shirtless boys
intent on something they lost

sara brant

Mum smiles as the sand
slips through enchanted fingers....
One eye on the tide

a scent of evening
the sound of one hand
carrying magnolias

Helen Buckingham

tawny owl
with a chorus of sparrows
in a tree above the highway

out-of-breath
in the wild of bindweed
pungent rootstalks

Raffael de Gruttola

8

HAIKU ON THE WIND

The excitement is all due to haiku. The Japanese poetry form is gaining momentum in the West like a puffball caught on the wind, creating a stir among poets like no other brief, but serious, form has ever enjoyed.

The brevity of the form may not be its only attraction. In the light of increased interest in environmental and peace issues, haiku seems a most effective and timely instrument to tug at the social conscience. Could this be the reason that haiku, the national pride of Japanese poets since the 1600s, has become so popular of late in the West?

Ezra Pound and other imagist poets attempted to introduce haiku to the West early this century. However, it was not until British poet R.H. Blyth produced four volumes simply entitled HAIKU in 1949 that western poets showed interest in the form.

When English-speaking writers became interested, it was apparent that the form would have to be tailored accordingly. First of all, the language difference posed problems, not only in the translation process from Japanese to English but in the physical aspect of the poem itself.

As most poets know, a traditional haiku has seventeen syllables. In Japanese however, a syllable is permitted only one consonant while a long vowel is equal to two syllables. So a 17-syllable Japanese haiku is half as short as the equivalent 17-syllable poem in English. This also affects the breath length.

As well, a Japanese haiku has only five to six words as opposed to the twelve or thirteen in English, so an English haiku adhering to Japanese presentation (written in one line) would run out of space. An English adaptation was in order and thus the three-lined 5/7/5 form was born.

Difficulties nevertheless remained for the western haiku enthusiast. As Eric Amann [1] points out, it was a formidable task for western poets to set aside the usual poetic devices in order to write acceptable haiku. Eventually poets learned that the successful haiku is void of simile, metaphor, rhyme and personification and never makes a statement.

Over the years the haiku's appearance has changed. Today everything from one to five line as well as experimental haiku can be found in leading haiku journals. This is also true of Japanese haiku.

Despite the modifications, perhaps the Japanese master and creator of the form, Matsuo Basho, would be pleased, if only because the basic spirit of haiku remains as strong, if not stronger, than ever.

Even Basho was unable to provide a definitive definition of haiku, but basically it is a moment of intense revelation and/or spiritual reward - a sudden awareness, an exclamation of vision/thought/emotion easily overlooked by those who do not exercise the "haiku eye".

The image often appears to be simple and unimportant, but by looking deeper, one is rewarded with a universe of wisdom. In other words, it is a personal communion between moment and observer. Therefore, each person (depending on their personal experience) may see/find completely different meanings in the same haiku.

"By looking deeper" is a statement that contradicts the masters of Japanese haiku who insisted that a haiku simply "is", that it has no other meaning. Discussing early haiku, Rod Willmot [2] points out "the reader was not supposed to admit to seeing any trace of meaning (in a haiku)". The working word here is "was": the haiku has changed, has been liberated so that the recipient can respond more humanely and naturally.

Because of the vast changes, a neophyte who delves into the numerous authoritative opinions, rules and studies of the form, can be overwhelmed. Analysis of haiku, on the other hand, can sometimes best explain. Consider this one-line haiku by Canadian poet, George Swede: [3]

October crumbles   in my hand

As a Northerner, "October" means vivid leaf colours of autumn: "crumbles" suggests fallen leaves, perhaps windgathered at the base of familiar trees: "in my hand" makes me an active/imaginative part of the haiku as I pick up a handful of once red (my choice) leaves that are now dry and brown. As I close my hand around the dried leaves, they crumble, gifting me with a sweet earthy scent. (The reader draws upon experience/knowledge to sharpen the image, to relate to it).

Apart from the active/visual/sensual participation, does this haiku offer anything else? Thinking deeper, I am aware that October represents not only a moment in, but the entire month — a month of magnificent colour/beauty/sun/rain/wind capsulated into one handful of leaves. The power of that simple act astonishes; in that small moment, I have the ability to do the impossible: to hold October, to hold time itself.

And yet, I am humbled: the leaves and I are alike: someday I too, after having served this world, will "crumble" and turn to dust in Mother Earth's hand. Despite the finality of this realisation, I am aware that dust serves the global system, is a very real part of existence. The thought comforts, emphasises my contributing (albeit small) importance to the planet, even after death.

So, on the one hand, the author is reminding me that, yes, humankind is important and powerful, but Nature is true master, existing within and without a time frame. And all living things invariably return to her safe keeping.

Brevity is a must in successful haiku. The haikuist works diligently to pare a poem to the bare essentials. A striking example is US poet Alexis Rotella's two-liner: [4]

> Seashell
>
> by God

Here, the image of a seashell, perhaps glistening wet on a sandy beach, or sitting on a kitchen shelf or coffee-table comes into focus. The mind caresses the rough/smooth exterior, follows the curves of beige/pink/pale orange that move toward the smooth mouth of the shell. Lifting it to the mind's "ear" one again hears the sea. Memories fill the shell, rush like warm sea-water. An overwhelming thought: this shell, this simple yet complex creation was actually crafted by God...and it belongs. It's important! Therefore so am I. The tremendous difference between the seashell versus the unlimitedness, the allness of God. The contrast startles and humbles.

Although three-line haiku remain the most popular, we can see a variety of syllable(s) per line, each line arranged interestingly so as to complement/intensify the image, as in the haiku that has immortalised the late Nicholas Virgilio: [5]

> lily:
> out of the water ...
> out of itself

Simple? Deceptively so. But go deeper with the image and see what happens: the lily ... white, perfect and beautiful, as it stands in cool green/blue water, comfortable and important in its natural habitat, has been snapped/pulled/cut away from its environment by a violent, selfish act. The flower is no longer independent and free: it has been robbed of its life-force, its natural place in the universal system. No longer in control of its life, it is dying (out of itself).

11

There is a deep sadness and a resentment at the thought of a defenceless flower being violently uprooted, forced into an unfamiliar environment due to the self-serving desires of another. The haiku suggests to me the vulnerability of the innocent/meek in our society, strong versus weak, and an entire range of social images. What we have is not just the simple image of a lily plucked from the water, but a story in a story in a story...

Haiku may appear simple, but each has an intricate network of imagery, beauty, simplicity and intensity that makes it unique as well as challenging. The fact that a haiku offers subtle hints, and in as few words as possible, urging the reader to supply what is not written/said, makes it exciting and fresh.

The successful haiku has an element of surprise that imprints itself on the reader so it's not too soon forgotten. Some readers have compared it to finding a golden nugget or having cold water flung into the face. Through a haiku's brevity and depth, one not only joins hands with all living things and the universal system, but cradles/nurtures them as well.

There are some who believe that through haiku, World Peace can be realised. Perhaps it's not as far-fetched as it seems. Given that haiku now is written (and appreciated) throughout the world and that haiku poets are in close communication with their world and universe, there seems little doubt that they may well understand and respect the meaning of peace and harmony far better than most others.

Elizabeth St Jacques

[1] Eric Amann: "**The Wordless Poem**". *Haiku Canada* 1969, 1978
[2] Rod Willmot: "**Essay on Haiku**". *Haiku Canada* 1987
[3] George Swede, *Origins* Vol.12 No.1
[4] Alexis Rotella, *Modern Haiku* Vol.XVIII No.3
[5] Nicholas A. Virgilio, *American Haiku* No.2 (by permission of author's brother, Tony Virgilio)

In water chasm
Titanic decomposes
nature over man

it takes the biscuit
crumbles and gobbles it then
flies off satisfied

Noel King

Bats rustle in thatch
Squirrels find their winter horde
Summer sun is gone

Birds twitter and feed
Kestrels strike from wintry skies
Garden has no birds

Jean Lloyd

my old neighbour
and his bent-over shadow —
buds just visible

Greek village church —
on the door of the crypt
election flyers

H. F. Noyes

A smile lights her eyes
In the picture on the wall
The smile always young.

A tiger stretches
Camouflaged in jungle grass
Its prey unaware.

Tommy Frank O'Connor

White dogroses climb
in curlicues on a pine,
needles thread petals.

Tombstones of trees
lie in grass and wild briars —
halfrisen shadows.

Ann Egan

FØROYAR

Faroe Island Poems

knots of time unravel
in endless afternoons
on an empty ocean

beneath the dark cliff
a thousand shades of silver
lift and fall in turn

my mountain primrose
threads an old, forgotten road
with tiny, glad buds

a mackerel shoal,
dark cloud on the blue-black sea:
a squall of white wings

owl call in an empty valley
darkens the grass
beneath a storm cloud

at Kirkja, patient waves
roll the beach pebbles, murmuring —
sea   wind   tomb

so close to the gods
their cloaks of red, green and gold
almost touch your face

Lesley Harrison

INVITATION TO THE WORLD OF HAIKU

Introduction

Before illustrating the mechanics of haiku, I should like to mention "haikai" which today is called "renku", the root of haiku. Nowadays the art is considered a creation of the individual, but renku is a literary art created by a group of poets called "renju". The history of haikai is uncertain, but it was originally a kind of "waka", a traditional style of poetry written in 5-7-5-7-7 syllables. The history of waka goes back to mythological times. Poets eventually divided it into two categories; one is humourous and came to be called haikai and the rest remained as waka.

Since the early 1900s haikai came to be called renku by the poet Takahama-Kyoshi (1874-1959). The first line of renku, written in 5-7-5 syllables called "hokku", gradually became popularised and finally separated from renku to be called haiku. Masaoka-Shiki (1867-1902) is the most notable poet in this "New Haiku" movement. He has insisted that the art must be a creation of the individual.

Rules of Haiku

Haiku is known as a brief poetic form written in 5-7-5 syllables; in English it is usually written in three lines. A seasonal word is essential in composition. Today's science and technology unfortunately are causes for neglecting the seasonal word.

a ra u mi ya	5	Here high roaring sea:-
sa do ni yo ko to o	7	Toward the Sado Island,
a ma no ga wa	5	A calm stream of Galaxy.

This is a typical work of Basho (1644-1694), an outstanding teacher of haiku; 5-7-5 syllables with seasonal word "a ma no ga wa", autumn.

However, haiku is not so rigid that it does not accept a change in form - if it is accompanied by creativity.

ka re e da ni	5	Lonesome resting crow:
ka ra su no to ma ri ke ri	9	On a leafless tree top tall
a ki no ku re	5	Autumn evening glow.

This is also a composition of Basho, but written in 5-9-5 syllables. Even such an authority as Basho has written like this, so 5-7-5 is not the "Golden Rule". Basho also wrote the same thought as follows:

ka re e da ni	5	On a leafless bough,
ka ra su no to ma ri ta ru ya	10	A crow has alighted:
a ki no ku re	5	Autumn evening glow.
ka re e da ni	5	On the skeleton bough
i no to ma ri ta ri ya	8	A crow is resting alone,
a ki no ku re	5	Autumn evening glow.

But we must recognise that even though the syllables are extended or shortened, the haiku must not sound unrhythmical. When haiku is written in more than 5-7-5 syllables, Japanese call it "ji a ma ri", meaning over-syllables. In contrast, when it is written in fewer syllables it is called "ji ta ra zu" Both "ji a ma ri" and "ji ta ra zu" are OK, but it is preferable to write in 5-7-5 because this structure in Japanese is used not only in haiku but also for waka and even in "kabuki" dialogue. It must be said that this metrical form gives the listener the most rhythmical feeling.

However, non-Japanese must be aware that Japanese syllabication is different from other languages. In Japanese, long vowels are counted as two syllables: Tokyo is To*o*kyo*o, four syllables, not two as in English. This method of scansion is applied throughout the prosody of the Japanese language.

Punctuation

There is no punctuation in haiku; the meaning of a haiku is dependent on the reader's interpretation. Japanese has no personal determination in verbs; the distinction between singular and plural is omitted. Eventually there is a possibility of different interpretation for whoever reads. This makes Japanese the most ideal language for poetry, but it also makes translation into other languages extremely difficult.

Seasonal Word

Whilst nowadays there is a tendency to omit the seasonal word, in classic haiku it was one of the important rules. Japan is a diverse climatic island country with four distinct seasons and in haiku these are clearly delineated according to the lunar calendar:

New Year:	The New Year Season
Spring:	February, March, April
Summer:	May, June, July
Autumn:	August, September, October
Winter:	November, December, January

We often consult a special dictionary called "saijiki", which describes things by season. Everything is classified by season: flowers, birds, fishes, and so on. Almost everything has its season in haiku. One reason for the current neglect of the seasonal word might be that today's poets no longer regard the seasons as they once did.

Ki re ji

Another important factor in haiku is "ki re ji", often described in the West as "cutting word", because it indicates a change of verbal continuum where it is placed.

Pattern 1

a ra u mi ya	Here high roaring sea:-
sa do ni yo ko to o	Toward the Sado Island,
a ma no ga wa	A calm stream of Galaxy.

"ya" in this case, gives a sense of expectation for coming action. "a ra u mi": high roaring sea is a talking point or eye catcher, "What's there?" may be in the reader's mind. So, ya is the word to draw this expectation; sometimes it also gives a sense of exclamation: it comes at the end of the first five syllables. In English it is expressed with an exclamation mark.

Pattern 2

shi ra tsu yu mo	Bush-clover is swaying!
ko bo sa nu ha gi no	So gently in the autumn breeze:
u ne ri ka na	White dew on the leaves.

"ka na" is an expression of deep feeling, or sense of exclamation. It comes at the end of seven syllables or at the end of the last five syllables.

Pattern 3

ka re e da ni	On a leafless bough,
ka ra su no to ma ri ke ri	A crow has alighted:
a ki no ku re	Autumn evening glow.

"ke ri" gives a sense of conclusion, sometimes it gives definition or confirmation, and is placed at the end of the seven or last five syllables to give a certain dignity to the sentence. To express the sense of "ki re ji" in another language is very difficult, but without this I fear a haiku in English becomes merely a short poem. For the sake of ki re ji haiku should make poets and readers more profound. To write haiku in English one has to know how to express this sense of ki re ji, otherwise the poem will lose its haiku personality. Haiku is written in 5-7-5 syllables, but, as ki re ji shows, it can be divided into two parts.

Pattern 1

a ra u mi ya		part A
sa do ni yo ko to o	}	part B
a ma no ga wa	}	

Pattern 2

ka re e da ni	}	part A
ka ra su no to ma ri ke ri	}	
a ki no ku re		part B

Pattern 3

shi ra tsu yu mo
ko bo sa nu ha gi no
u ne ri ka na ....

When ki re ji is placed at the end of the last syllables, it cannot be divided. The most suitable interpretation of rhythm in my opinion seems to be

/ — / — /
/ — / — / — /
/ — / — /

possibly rhymed at the end of the first and third lines.

Patterns

ko no mi chi ya	No passerby,
yu ku hi to na shi ni	On this distant travelling road:
a ki no ku re	Autumn makes me sigh.

Seasonal words: a ki no ku re = autumn   ki re ji: ya

me i ge tsu ya	Beautiful moon light:-
i ke o me gu ri te	I walked round and round the pond,
yo mo su ga ra	Almost through the night.

Seasonal words: me i ge tsu = autumn   ki re ji: ya

Basho (1644-1694)

yu ki to ke te	Snow has melted away -
mu ra ip- pa i no	Every corner of the village
ko do mo ka na	Children, joyfully playing.

Seasonal words: yu ki to ke = spring   ki re ji: ka na

ha ru sa me ya	Pouring spring-time rain:-
a hi ru yo chi yo chi	Ducklings are toddling joyfully
ka do a ru ki	A water filled lane.

Seasonal words: ha ru sa me = spring   ki re ji: ya

Issa (1763-1877)

a ki no ya ma ni	To climb up the mountain:
no bo re ba sa ra ni	It becomes more higher -
te n ta ka shi	The autumn sky.

Seasonal words: a ki   ki re ji: none

chi ni o chi te	Fallen on the ground,
na o u tsu ku shi ki	Yet it is beautiful as it is:
mo mi ji ka na	A red leaf of maple.

Seasonal words: mo mi ji   ki re ji: ka na

Shojiro Shibasaki (1912 -)

José Civasaqui

19

Child feeding goldfish
kneeling on a bamboo bridge —
floating up and down

Robert Leechford

The moonlight
streaming over her fingers,
a bowl of milk, spilt.

Joy Yourcenar

it cost a lifetime
of suffering to sit by
this fire with this book

birds fly overhead
as I think "how beautiful"
they're already gone

Norton Hodges

Bare feet in wet grass,
jumping froglets, wakening sun;
tickle, tickle, hop.

Pat Mitchell

for miles and miles
trees hung with fog
crowd the highway

Joanna Ashwell

Under crescent moon
at twilight, wild ponies
grazing on the marsh

green willows tracing
full moon over Manhattan
their leaves — bird shadows

W. Luther Jett

PROBLEMS OF TRANSLATION

With haiku, when every single word is of vital importance, the quality of the translation is obviously crucial. Literal translation is often not possible and many different versions of the same Japanese haiku appear in English. It is interesting to compare them, by looking at the poem by Basho most often quoted as an initial example of haiku.

Firstly a translation by Lucien Stryk: [1]

> On the dead limb
> squats a crow —
> autumn night.

Stryk notes that this haiku has eighteen syllables in the original. Following the train of thought that English haiku should contain fewer than the standard seventeen syllables, he retains just ten. The transliteration is given as

> Kareeda ni
> Karasu no tomarikeri
> Aki no kure

Personally I find the word "squat" inappropriate for a bird. Nobuyuki Yuasa [2] offers a four line version:

> A black crow
> Has settled himself
> On a leafless tree,
> Fall of an autumn day.

The last line here bothers me; the word "fall" inadvertently adding an American translation of "autumn"!

The *Penguin Book of Japanese Verse* [3] settles for:

> On a bare branch
> A rook roosts:
> Autumn dusk.

Though perhaps just a little too abrupt, it provides an interesting contrast to the previous four-liner. A comprehensive introduction to this book does suggest a very careful consideration of the Japanese language and its development. Nevertheless I am unhappy with the alliteration in the second line.

Harold G. Henderson [4] gives us:

> On a withered branch
> a crow has settled ...
> autumn nightfall.

In addition to this different line arrangement in English, he quotes a transliteration in one-line Japanese style:

> Kare eda ni karasu no tomarikera aki no kure.

Within an appendix which deals with the problems of translation, Henderson admits that "translated haiku can only very seldom convey the full force of the originals" and that no translation can be absolutely perfect. He advises "If, in reading translations, you come across a haiku that does not convey to you any emotion at all, do not blame yourself or the poet. Blame it on the translator!" Perhaps a little harsh, as he himself suggests that we, as readers, must be prepared to work on haiku ourselves.

Makoto Ueda [5] in a study previously published by Twayne in 1970 gives us:

> On a bare branch
> A crow is perched —
> Autumn evening.

Interestingly he describes the form as rather free, consisting of 5-10-5 syllables in the original version and 5-9-5 in the final version.

More recently we have a translation by Atsuo Nagagawa [6]

> On a withered branch
> A crow is perching —
> Autumn evening

and from James Kirkup:[7],

> Upon a dead branch
> a crow comes and perches --
> evening in autumn

For me, the most effective translation remains the first I read, that by Kenneth Yasuda [8]

> On a withered bough
> A crow alone is perching;
> Autumn evening now.

It is perhaps significant that in his introduction Yasuda states that the examples given are offered "not as translations, but as haiku in English." His interpretation produces, presumably more by accident than design, a rhyming line, not normally associated with haiku. Others, no doubt, will feel differently about these alternatives, and it may be that the impact of my first encounter was bound to be lessened on subsequent encounters. I am quite sure even more versions exist!

Bruce Clark

[1] Lucien Stryk, ON LOVE AND BARLEY: HAIKU OF BASHO, Penguin 1985
[2] Nobuyuki Yuasa, THE NARROW ROAD TO THE DEEP NORTH, 1966
[3] Geoffrey Bownas & Anthony Thwaite, THE PENGUIN BOOK OF JAPANESE VERSE, 1964
[4] Harold G. Henderson, HAIKU IN ENGLISH, Tuttle, 1967
[5] Makoto Ueda, "Matsuo Basho", Kodanshka International, 1982
[6] *The Haiku Quarterly* No.1 Winter 1990
[7] *Blithe Spirit* No.1, 1990
[8] Kenneth Yasuda, THE JAPANESE HAIKU, Tuttle, 1957

reaching the top step
he pauses to remember
what he came up for

scuffed trainers and dirty jeans
neatly covered —
the choirboy changes

Andrew Detheridge

Autumn light;
thistledown quivers
in a spider's web

café à la terrasse —
her bookmark
a red carnation

John Crook

After four days lost
In the mountains I notice
My thighs are still plump

autumn afternoon nap
a broom
lying in the garden

remembering this morning
soap, melting away
in my bathtub

in the bowl
a tight bunch of grapes
resisting her fingers

MTC Cronin

her red lips
a lasting impression
on an empty cup

whispering
but still
the echo

twilight stroll
— locks turning
behind me

stuck in traffic
the incessant smile
of a billboard blonde

Giovanni Malito

forest hike in spring
on the ground fresh cougar scat
bristling with deer hair

moss-hung trees
a deer moves into
the hunter's silence

in the pocket
of his woodshed coveralls
a nest of deer mice

snowman
in the parking lot
anatomically correct

Winona Baker

On the Red Hymn Book
a ladybird or dried blood?
Remembrance Sunday.

this cold night
nothing moves
but stars

Carol A. Coiffait

Jason Sanford Brown

spring ice on white
Chiricahua riverstones
Geronimo's bones

on a wind whipped ridge
the butterfly suns itself
in a bear track

Thomas Fitzsimmons

rush hour traffic
a jogger
passes us all

on the lily pad
playing leap frog —
two blue dragonflies

Jean M. Aloe

REFLECTIONS ON HAIKU

Long before the emergence of space travel and cyberspace, a select group probed their limited universe for inspiration and enlightenment. They were the Zen priest-poets who developed the art of haiku.

In the traditional format, a haiku portrays a moment in nature, not always expressing just a pretty picture in words, but a meaningful concept that the poet wishes to express. Most of the original haiku poets adhered to the Buddhist doctrine that all creatures and things are fleeting images in the parade of life, yet part of the universal brotherhood of creation. The work of these poets usually reflected this philosophy and formed a pattern for serious haiku writers to this day.

The modern haiku poet, like Basho and the other founders of the genre, must always be alert to the endless scenes of life around them for inspiration in creating these small written gems, which celebrate the importance of a tiny bit of the universe.

While many poets and editors today have deviated from the traditional 5-7-5 pattern, meeting the challenge of finding just the right seventeen syllables to convey just the right ambience or feeling, is the mark of true creativity.

Jean M. Kahler

cold watery sun
sees tom cat waiting for cream —
the milkman cometh

Christine England

broiled salmon
the cat makes a leap
for my lunch

hortensia anderson

pendulum tail curves
as the cat walks the tightrope
of the garden fence

Andrew Detheridge

pied wagtail on lawn
sleek black kitten stalking it
— not a chance

Gerald England

on our tangled legs
the cat kicking
fleas into the bed

MTC Cronin

Bird watching —
two cats' heads move
back and forth

John Crook

driving through mist
a white cat waits
by a mailbox

Winona Baker

dead heat...
cat watching mouse
slowly slinking by

Giovanni Malito

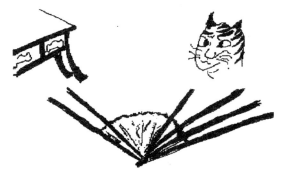

SABI IN HAIKU

The Japanese word "sabi" expresses a uniquely vital element in the haiku tradition. Though the concept, like much in Japanese art, is so elusively subtle as to afford no easy accessibility to Western minds, let us at the very least be willing to confront the mystery and paradox of the term. We are told by R.H. Blyth [1] that "what can be said is not sabi". That imposes no obstacle to a haijin who understands Zen "wordlessness" as an eloquent form of communion. Take Kishu's [2]

> Autumn dusk -
> without a cry
> a jackdaw passes

The deepest truths are imageless; they emanate from the unexpressed, the wordless aspect of haiku — however essential each word may be:

> how silently
> the wave-tossed log is beached
> and snow-flaked
> ### Geraldine C. Little [3]

The mystery of sabi intensifies when I quote from Basho: [4] "Where there is no sabi, there will be sadness." Then sabi cannot encompass what we usually mean by sadness. Rather it goes beyond happiness/sadness to the lonely quality which each thing has in its singular existence, when observed from a state of detachment. Sabi loneliness, according to Alan Watts [5], is in seeing things "as happening 'by themselves' in miraculous spontaneity." He gives as example Buson's

> Evening breeze -
> water lapping against
> the heron's legs.

The great surprise is that when we immerse ourselves in nature, an isolated particularity becomes to us, for the moment, all things. Sabi loneliness is a state in which, having nothing, we have all. Note the proximity in English of "aloneness" to "all-oneness". It is a state of which

Blyth [6] says we "do not pick and choose what we are to rejoice and weep with." "It" chooses "us":

> winter hill -
> alone together
> with wind and stars
> ### H.F. Noyes [7]

William J. Higginson [8] describes sabi as "beauty with a sense of loneliness in time." A fine example is:

> Who can be awake
> the lamp still burning -
> cold rain at midnight
> ### Ryota [9]

Despite undertones of melancholy in sabi, the more desolate aspects of our human condition are, traditionally, sublimated. The sadness of transience is transcended when we go unresisting with the flow of constant change. The loneliness that afflicts us all is thus resolved, or at least for the moment dissolved in interfusion with all around us. Tombo's [10] unspoken sadness over the loss of her son is overwhelmed by her sense of the delicate beauty of one transient phenomenon:

> A hot summer wind -
> shadows of the windmill blades
> flow over the grass

In the depth and breadth of a true haijin spirit such as Basho's, life's suffering and its sublime moments of beauty and serenity are perfectly reconciled:

> A rough sea! —
> Stretched out over Sado
> The Milky Way. [11]

But sabi arises, above all, with the observation of the garden variety of "insignificant" detail that makes up our ordinary lives, where sabi is not

29

in the beauty, but rather the beauty is in the sabi. Indeed sabi is often best expressed through the "lonesome" bareness of a "poverty-stricken" style:

> Visiting the graves:
> The old dog
> Leads the way.
>
> **Issa** [12]

However much a consensus on the meaning of sabi may elude us, a humble viewpoint of selfless detachment seems to lead us into its realm of truth:

> Resting...
> the sagging fence
> goes on up the hill
>
> **Foster Jewell** [13]

H. F. Noyes

[1] R.H.Blyth, EASTERN CULTURE
[2] Blyth, HAIKU Vol.III
[3] *Frogpond*, Nov.1987
[4] Blyth, EASTERN CULTURE
[5] Alan Watts, THE WAY OF ZEN
[6] Blyth, EASTERN CULTURE
[7] *Amber*, Spring 1989
[8] William J. Higginson & Penny Harter, THE HAIKU HANDBOOK
[9] Blyth, HAIKU Vol.IV
[10] *Dragonfly*, July 1973
[11] translated by Dana B. Young
[12] Blyth, HAIKU Vol.IV
[13] *Virtual Image*, Summer-Fall 1982

it's a day of rest
   again she prepares dinner
unable to stop

drinking too much booze
   he blames her for everything
even now she's gone

blue Delphiniums
   tints of clothes my mother loves
and resents sewing

on death row
   sunlight stabs walls
hits bars hard

Joan Payne Kincaid

I breathe
the same air as
those sparrows

oh rainbow
not being where I see you
colourful fraud

summer evening
we still linger outside
the blackbird and I

your own way
without knowing the map
you choose your track

along the sky
a swarm of dots on the move
to somewhere

going together
to where the one has to leave
the other behind

Max Verhart

rear view mirror
the sky filled with clouds
is filling it

long distance —
asking the wrong grandchild
about his birthday

in a country store
at the end of a blue lake
postcards but no bread

wrinkled pond
not stopping to add
my reflection

Leatrice Lifshitz

31

Picnickers —
Mob of cows
Circling

The subject drifts
In a lost conversation
Dry leaf tossed by the wind

Vanessa Proctor

Seasons change   strong winds
sticks, paper, string for kites used
instead for poetry

japan   same morning
same signature haiku and
takeover clincher

Michael Grove

under the covers
making elaborate plans
for the eclipse

climbing down
feeling the avalanche
in each stone

Thom Williams

running child's laughter
red ribbon bouncing in hair
confused hummingbird

branch with many twigs
garden wet from last night's rain
I shake my shower

Vaughn Banting

on arriving home
trails across the garden snow
foraging bird food

passing clouds over
manhattan's concrete valley
heart in liverpool

Jim Bennett

UNFREEZING THE MOMENT

after silence
other words
unfreezing the moment

Shanghai — the waterfront. A tall, debonair character is being pursued through the teeming street. Three vast, evil henchmen are closing in, sunlight glinting on their shaven pates as he draws from his jacket pocket — a pipe. Lights it, exhales, a slight smile plays about his lips as... for a moment all is still - the still, still point of the turning world. [1] It is, as the voice-over to the advert tells us, that 'Condor' moment, or almost as Eliot would have said. "...the unattended/moment in and out of time/the distraction fit" [2]

From the ridiculous to the sublime? Perhaps. But any definition of a haiku will give you something related to both, about "recording the essence of a moment keenly perceived" [3] — probably the one thing that we haiku writers agree on, apart from brevity.

This is the haiku moment, when perception of some piece of reality becomes a moment of contemplation, an event charged with significance; it is the intersection of the timeless with time where we see into the heart of things. The poetry of haiku involves a powerfully economical communication of this experience, or rather, presenting it so that the reader may relive it for himself. As Van den Heuvel asserts "the reader must be an equal partner in the creative process." [4] Shelving the question of the reader's responsibility for the present, we may say, "So far, so good." These moments of insight are devoutly to be wished, as times when we are most intensely alive, however many hatchetmen surround us. Indeed, "Ridiculous the waste sad time/stretching before and after." [5]

But what more might poetry do? Is it only to be concerned with moments, fragments of our lives — freeze-framed, the blink of a shutter — however brilliant? If this is as far as haiku can go, is it enough, or should we be looking elsewhere, too? Consider a potted history of English poetry to date, and the range of interests therein. Ask then what answers haiku give to the needs our traditions have dealt with so far.

The first poetry was incantatory, the pulsating lists of Caedmon's names for God, in the style of the epic stories of the Anglo-Saxons. Later, 3082 lines lauded the exploits of Beowulf in packed, formulaic lines built on stress rhythms, intensively alliterative. Narrative needs this length and space for compounding actions and scenes of events, whole worlds imaginatively created with corroborative detail and the memorable speeches of boasting and rabble-rousing. Creeping in, too, the moralising tendency of the new Christianity, that requires space first to recount and then interpret. Elsewhere, pre-Conquest, was the elegiac mode — describing, analysing, lamenting the passing of the old order. Some quirky little riddles, besides fragments of gnomic wisdom, are the nearest we come to compactness here.

With the Norman invasion came new continental influences, bringing Romance and the elegant lyrics of courtly love. Full end rhyme and stanzaic form joined the native tradition, giving us "Gawain", beside the love songs. Love, of course, needs at least enough space to list the loved one's sterling qualities, besides a comprehensive unfolding of passion. Chaucer took up the dramatic strain and expanded it to give us verse in which psychologically convincing characters came alive through dialogue, interaction and description. The heroic couplet, of rhyming counted syllables in metrical lines, became a powerful tool of expression and argument here — capable of both the rhetorical figures of Classical origin and the flexibility of natural speech; from sententiae to chat.

After native experimentation and consolidation [e.g. Skelton, interestingly, unusually short] came further influence at the Renaissance from the continent. Foremost was the Italian sonnet, with its fine balance of length and concentration answering the English interest in both the argumentative and the lyrical. In the hands of the Elizabethan and Jacobean dramatists, blank verse became the medium of tremendous force and architecture. As the awareness of Greek and Roman playwrights grew, so did the grandeur of the verse, encompassing comedy and the great tragic themes, besides the newfound interests in science, philosophy, travel &c. The language grew under this pressure — from Marlowe and Shakespeare the intense, extended and various imagery; the powerful tension of Latinate and Germanic diction; the poetry of argument and analysis; the depths and heights of passion, and a complex new psychology.

On, then, to the extraordinary visions of the Metaphysicals, their densely packed paradoxical arguments moving poetry into intellectual wordgames, too. Beyond them, the central power of Milton who gave us Eden and the ways of God in twelve books, a new epic voice, whose blank verse sounded trumpets. Next, the endless variations on classical form before the Golden Age of Pope and Dryden, their urbanely barbed wit and philosophical treatises finding the perfect vehicle in the closed thought patterns of the heroic couplet. Thereafter the lovely excesses of the Romantics, the lyrics, odes, Wordsworth's spiritual journeys and Coleridge's mystical narrative. Through the Nineteenth century's ever expanding interests [fireside Tennyson and bizarre Hopkins] to the explosion of individualism. *Vers libre* broke the metrical and rhyming mould. And into the multitudinous experiments of the 20th cent: Symbolists, Vorticists, Imagists [getting closer to haiku], Georgians, Angry Young Men, The Movement, Minimalists — and Betjeman flourishing by Ginsberg, and Larkin with Auden. Eliot, of course. And then all the outpourings of the last thirty or so years.......

This is what English poetry has been and done — and in its very versatility I see a response to actual needs, as much as any poet-led initiative in developing form. The personal, subjective and confessional lies down with the objective and analytical; with polemic and political; the satirical and the didactic with light verse and the devotional; with argumentative, political; with lyrical, with narrative, with dramatic... the Westerner sees himself as free to pursue any form and any content. He can write as well about kitchen tables as Weltschmerz, the high old themes as well as bus-stop platitudes. This is an attitude to the world and art which is dynamic, progressive and individualistic: we know only the artistic bounds we are prepared to acknowledge. By contrast, the Japanese haiku is traditionally a conservative and restrained vehicle, and whilst based squarely in focus on things real, is nevertheless largely contemplative and reactive. In haiku proper we are moreover restricted to the topic of man's relation to nature, with the requirement of the season "*jion*" as one of seventeen syllables. Senryu is allowed more latitude in tone and theme, but consequently regarded by many as a lesser form. Besides the restriction of content is the obvious one of length — how much can actually be given to a reader in the poetic equivalent of one breath or less? As with all minimalist art, the onus falls on the audience/reader to supply imaginative flesh to the bare bones offered: the meaning is implicit — there are neither the words nor the philosophy to spell out any vision. Cor van den Heuvel said "These haiku moments await only your contribution of awareness" [6]. That "only" is something of an under-statement: many readers find that the haiku does NOT speak to them but is a closed statement of the obvious. It may be felt to be banal and lacking the magic that is often associated with poetry; whereas a longer poem offers more clues, more development and further imagery to enable communication to work. I was once asked to find a poem to read at a funeral - this was a need no haiku could fulfil.

If the meaning may be limited, the music certainly is so. The potential for rhythm, for example, can hardly be exploited over the linear equivalent of less than a heroic couplet. Indeed, the general dynamics of music — the possibility of crescendo and diminuendo, and the structuring of blocks of sound — are hardly possible. One can, of course, employ the individual devices of sound in a haiku to good effect (alliteration, assonance, onomatopoeia &c), but they do have a tendency to stand out rather, and dominate. Ultimately, haiku is a matter of the simplest presentation of experience, with the least artfulness — its greatest strength, and, I would argue, its greatest limitation.

Perhaps all this seems like an Aunt Sally: maybe haiku is not seriously expected by anyone to fulfil more than a circumscribed role [although I have heard writers proudly proclaim that they write nothing else]. Perhaps given sufficient latitude in form and content, it could do much more. Many of us have argued [7] for its fuller potential to be realised by the liberalisation of the form — the shift from the 5-7-5 model to other patterns of generally fewer syllables over other than three lines; the use of types of sequences; more [c. 31 syllable] tanka; the use of titles; omission of season word or any statutory break; the use of rhyme &c.

However, even if not liberalised, maybe it doesn't matter that the haiku only does certain things. We can accept it as yet another useful weapon for our raids on the inarticulate. The haiku is not the be-all and end-all of poetry; the frozen moment is not the centre of life, nor the sole object of writing. Any writer seduced into poetic contemplation of merely one's navel risks stultifying his art. What is worse, it would be elevating the minimalist poetic to an indefensible pedestal from which the "conventional" poet and Joe Public will rightly take pleasure in knocking it. We will do this precious form of writing no service by making inflated claims for it, and ourselves no good, if we become frozen into one way of seeing, and writing about, the world.

Geoffrey Daniel.

[1] T.S. Eliot, THE FOUR QUARTETS.
[2] ibid
[3] The Haiku Society of America.
[4] Cor van den Huevel, THE HAIKU ANTHOLOGY, Touchstone, 1986.
[5] T.S. Eliot, THE FOUR QUARTETS.
[6] Cor van den Huevel op cit
[7] *Blithe Spirit* No.4 1990

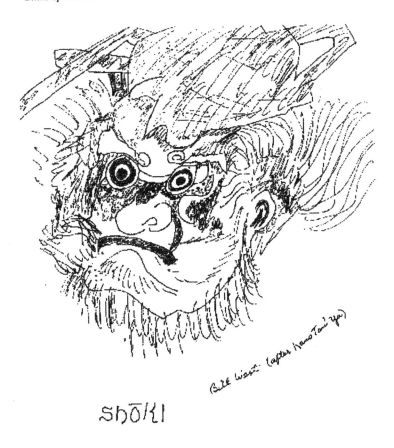

Bill West (after Hans Tani' yu)

SHŌKI

After the night storm
even the mud red puddles are
covered with red leaves

Jean M. Kahler

walking the trail
one crimson leaf
sticks to muddy boot

Michelle V. Lohnes

Early January.
Red Admiral on the wing —
Indian winter!

Colin Nixon

the old woman
next door —
still pruning her bushes

Del Doughty

ON THE MOON

linked haiku by Marlene Mountain (<) & Michelle V. Lohnes (>)

<   "gross insensitivity to beliefs . . human remains on the moon" [1]
>   bone worn driftwood curves into the dunes
<   jagged things appear in the snow that hangs around the shed
>   strung on a bent nail — crystal teardrop
<   a thin pane of nothing between birds at the feeder and me
>   news flash... dust clouds surrounding planets

>   cold night my shovel scrapes a path through the silence
<   possums on the tin roof trash bags i thought safe
>   discarded pines brown needles drop in piles along the curb
<   millennium smillennium
>   missing the art show old calendar still hangs on the wall
<   'teen-age mom barred' from honor society
>   target practice 'no trespassing' sign full of holes
<   bible-inspired web site fake blood & hit-list
>   silken threads spun between rose bud and thorn
<   wallpaper music tonight its emotional tug
>   old man's profile edges outward shadows in peeling layers
<   afternoon nap the guilt of cozy quilts

```
<   short-term memory loss fuses with middle-term memory loss
>   fingertips trace feathered prints in rock
<   older than 'lucy' of course the dig-guys hope it's a guy
>   string tied to stakes for climbing beans
<   when 'long tall sally' was in i still can't dance a lick
>   closet cleaning red spike heels unworn in the box
<   'two brides 97 ministers in lesbian protest wedding' 68 & 63
>   hand-painted sign trimmed in white organza
<   whatever it hides the sales pitch is 'not from concentrate'
>   aquarium life transparent eggs beneath jagged rocks
<   'honor killing' her brother proud he did it ashamed of her [2]
>   blood-lines blurred with each half sibling

>   stark night — edges softened through fogged windows
<   massive systems crash fixed humbled now by chills
>   icy roof heaves resonant cracks unseen above our heads
<   fragmented mind some spots of green in ungreen spots
>   jigsaw puzzle thousand piece forest strewn over the table
<   whether flowers bloom the odor of earth in my ears
```

Marlene Mountain & Michelle V. Lohnes

[1] Navajo president Albert Hale and Marlene Mountain
[2] incident in Pakistan

Red crayon
On white walls
Children's giggles

Vanessa Proctor

A flame flares briefly;
logs shift, settle in the grate
Wolf wind howls outside

Beryl Haigh

valentine's day
I buy myself
a box of chocolates

lesbian friend
also notices
the short skirt

Dennis Dutton

ON READING HAIKU [1]

The writing and the reading are two separate creative functions which form the single whole of a haiku. As writers we tend to feel we have done the entire thing when the moment of the haiku experience is captured and expressed on paper. Raymond Roseliep put it well [2] "As Auden and Valery before him said of the poem, no haiku is ever finished, it is only abandoned. So the reader keeps getting on where the poet got off." The brevity and surface simplicity of a haiku require the reader to put flesh on the bones of the moment's skeleton.

Let us "read" the following haiku.

> among the shadows
> a tiny yellow mushroom —
> waning autumn sun

Here the poet has expressed the moment of his awareness in purely visual terms. We immediately see a picture. As the Japanese master Basho has said, a haiku is simply what is happening in this place at this moment. The reader may think that once over lightly gives him this haiku, but repetition and slow reading will yield more. Harold J. Isaacson [3] remarked that one way to read haiku is to go through a number of haiku and choose one that seems of particular interest, memorise it and live with it in the mind for an entire day, thinking about it. He says that "slowly the mind will open towards the full force and sense of the content of it, which in that way will have the aspect of gradually revealing itself and manifesting to the one who thus puts his attention upon the haiku."

So we go back to the haiku, reading more slowly, more sensitively. Each of us will bring our own peculiar knowledge and experience to inhabit the words and so enter the world of the haiku.

I focus first on the mushroom, which is the chief image, and move forward to the sun. Here a texture is formed by the contrast between the size of the tiny mushroom and that of the sun overlain by the similarity of colour. The haiku is beginning to round out. Look closely at the third line. A waning moon is commonplace but here the uncommon use of "waning sun" enriches the experience. Here we have two objects both being themselves. But I wonder. Is the poet also telling us that the

40

mushroom IS the waning sun? Perhaps that is his main meaning. It doesn't matter to me for the two meanings merge in the fabric of the haiku. Going back to the opening line, which at first seemed introductory, I read it again — "among the shadows". I think of shadows, of kinds of shadows, of the quality of light and how the nothingness of shadows as a setting highlights the solidity of the mushroom with form and substance.

Such an analytical reading (though barely begun) is one way of entering a haiku. Having pulled it apart in this way, we can go back and read it again for pure enjoyment. In coming back to it at a later time we may find new facets, new depths. A good haiku will have growth quality.

What has this way of reading to do with the poet? Just this, that he too must become a reader after he has done the writing. The haiku must be written swiftly, intuitively while the awareness is fresh. To revise or satisfy himself that he has indeed captured the moment as skilfully as he can, he must look at it objectively, become a reader and lay aside, in so far as he can, the experience that prompted the haiku in order to see if his clues provide a satisfactory poem capable of giving the reader his own unique moment of perception.

Elizabeth Searle Lamb.

[1] Original version, *Wind Chimes* No.2 1981
[2] Raymond Roseliep, LISTEN TO LIGHT, Alembic Press 1980
[3] Masaoki Shiki, PEONIES KANA. A SELECTION OF HAIKU translated by Harold J. Isaacson, Theatre Arts Books 1972.

THE FURROW'S END

a traditional nijuin spring renku between: Sue Mill (<) and Ferris Gilli (>)

>	a clay road —	bobwhites in a line	hop from the ditch
<	at the furrow's end,	one faint hoofprint	
>	wedding reception	the bride kicks off	her borrowed shoes
<	from the valley head	the murmur of a clear waterfall	
>	hide-and-seek	under the full moon	shrieks of laughter
>	in the hammock's fold	a black widow	
<	the voodoo doll	dangles in the breeze	lightning tears the sky
>	mending his favorite jeans —	her careful stitches	
<	beside the bed	their discarded clothing	in a single pile
>	alien teeth fill the screen —	scattered popcorn	
<	the little boy	hefts a wooden sword —	his father's big grin
>	beach sign nailed to a post	no cars allowed — turtles nesting	
<	crescent moon in Scorpio	swaying orange lanterns	hold back the night
>	a crumbling outhouse	Virginia creeper bars the door	
<	rotten straw	scarecrow's right arm	lying limp on the ground
<	sparks spiral upward	from the cottage chimney	
>	secret recipe	from a worn notebook -	rotini in the soup
<	New Year's promise —	fingers crossed behind his back	
>	a soft humming	on Easter Sunday	bees in the dogwood
<	spring shower —	frog chorus fills the air	

Sue Mill & Ferris Gilli

---

reading old poets in bed

* * * * * * *

crickets fill in the rest

* * *

*

Jesse Glass

42

SF POETS EMBRACE SENRYU

"It's small because it has in it the only possible words, and not a single one over." So wrote Suzette Haden Elgin [1] introducing a short poem, "Moons". STAR LINE, founded in 1978, is the newsletter of the US-based Science Fiction Poetry Association. "Moons" seems to have been the first poem published in the magazine to follow the 5-7-5 syllable format. But Suzette, editor, a linguistics expert, author of many theoretical articles on poetry, a science fiction novelist and poet, does not describe the piece as haiku. Nor did she do so when another piece by the same author appeared in a later issue [2]

The SFPA has a tradition of challenging members to try different poetic forms, including such newly invented ones as the "quotella". In May 1981, when Robert Frazier set the next workshop his wording was unequivocal: "I am now open to submission of haiku, or tankas." Several members took up the challenge and their work was published. [3] No one, however, queried the use of the term haiku in an SF poetry context. A letter from Harry Davidov in response to a private letter from the then associate editor Gene Van Troyer began, a year later, a debate that was to continue strongly through two issues.

Davidov, after saying that Van Troyer's letter was the first time he had heard mention of "senryu", focuses on the "traditional seasonal references" of haiku and draws a clear moral for SF writers from the situation within two commonplace "off world" settings. "On a planet that doesn't have summer and fall and winter and spring, or in seasonless space, there are no such traditional references." He suggests ways round this problem: having "a spaceman/colonist recall memories of Earth" for example. Then, having said that "Fantasy or horror haiku might be possible" he throws down the gauntlet - "Can SF haiku be written - or are only SF senryu possible?"

In an appended editorial note, Van Troyer clarifies "Senryu are structurally identical to haiku, but lack seasonal referents." He also gives his own opinion on the question raised; "As to whether SF haiku are possible, yes, I think so, but not if they stand alone." This intriguing hint as to lack of "aloneness" was never clarified. His promised article on Japanese verse forms used in an SF context was never to appear.

A later issue [5] returns to the topic. Jonathan V. Post's ongoing series of articles about the relationship of poetry and Artificial Intelligence quotes researcher John Morris; [6] "The computer had produced some four thousand haikus. For one glorious month I was the world's most prolific poet." Post introduced this data in the context of discussing Coleridge's definition of poetry's essential quality - "maximum density — its untranslateability in words of the same language without injury to the meaning" [7] – a fascinating pre-echo of the words of Suzette Elgin.

Jane Helser, having taken up the challenge to produce an SF haiku, prefaced it with an eight line prose "Hypothesis" to the effect that Space itself has "seasons" of immense length — in crude terms, the Big Bang universe was basically hot, ours basically cold, and the process could well be cyclical. Copyright restrictions prevent me quoting this or other responses to the challenge but hopefully the "Hypothesis" allows one to sense the approach of the poems.

Suzette Elgin weighs in with an intriguing half-page piece; it offers an escape from over-simplified thinking about season, or maybe misplaced ingenuity is at work in her thinking. She propounds the idea that seasonal references refer not to seasons as such but to "a context established by convention... when a haiku mentions cherry blossoms, the reference is to ... a vast cultural construct that just INCLUDES springtime." Drawing parallels with examples in English like "the holly and the ivy", she explains the process at work as "a way of fitting equally vast chunks of information, almost emblematically, into the tight constraints of the haiku." Hence "The Japanese 'seasonal reference' hangs on the association tree ... all its parts protected from tampering" because it is of that class of cultural constructs "built over great spans of time by whole populations." She suggests, as a means of overcoming the near impossibility for the SF writer of artificially duplicating such a lengthy process, that an "existing construct (like Camelot)" be taken — "Just rotate it in literary space a bit."

Five poets took up the challenge in the next issue. Jane Yolen wrote in a letter "..the very 'lack' of seasons might be the point, equating that lack to death/distance from home/loss of earthness &c"

An article by David Lunde [8] discusses lyric poetry in general and the problems it poses in the context of SF which he says "has traditionally dealt with man as a whole rather than the individual." He goes on to say that "because haiku is one of the most purely lyrical forms ever developed," the problems are compounded and "this is probably the least appropriate form for the SF poet of any." He quotes definitions by Basho and others. Curiously the main one he chooses to paraphrase, that haiku "should express the nature of the particular in such a way as to define the essence of all creation through it ... a statement first of the unchanging, then the momentary, then the point of intersection between the two," could in fact be used to describe many aspects of SF itself. He concludes "It seems to me that all of these requirements" [having discussed "kigo" &c] "make the haiku such a restricted form that it is of little use not only for the science fiction poet but for any Western poet." Without expanding further on this provocative remark, he praises the aptness of senryu for the SF poet's purpose, stressing its freedom from the need for a Zen or mystical philosophical bedrock. "The senryu", says Lunde, "stops short with the particular and deals mostly in the failings and distortions, rather than the beauty of nature."

In a footnote to the article, Van Troyer points out that the pre-Basho haiku WAS "disreputable and vulgar", that "English lacks the syllabic structure which, in Japanese, makes the haiku what it is" and that the "kate-kotoba" or "pivot-words" of haiku, with their dual meanings, mean that "the pivot-word line of a haiku can be read as two lines contained in one".

Of the five poems, published in that issue, Lorraine Schein's with its laser image for the whiteness of an alien winter, though titled "Haiku," and Robert Medcalf's "Sunspots" with its fading of voices "across the void" seem definitely at the senryu side of the divide, even though too gentle in mood to be "the envenomed dart" kind of senryu so often contrasted with the "falling petal" of haiku.

Loretta Smith's leafless oaks are returned nostalgically to by "Aliens" though that word is ambiguous indeed. Here, a conclusion seems only "non-proven." Marsh's piece, conjuring a nova whose occurrence goes "unnoticed" by the dead winter foliage is, in my opinion, truly a haiku, while Lunde has in a way set out to prove his own thesis by writing of voyagers on the Milky Way, albeit in terms almost entirely those of Earth-bound river craft.

In "Star Line" the debate has been set aside these past sixteen years. Nonetheless I see growing signs today of a search for orthodoxy, rigidity, approved ways, in the wider context of Western haiku writing generally. Surely we can all learn from the SFPA members' exploration of the issue. They effectively concluded that in the senryu lay the appropriate liberating tool to free Western poets from the cramping constrictions of "wearing borrowed armour".

In the last couple of years there has been an upsurge of poems using the 5-7-5 form and having science-fictional content, on the Internet [9] as well as in magazines and SFanzines. For these the clumsy generic term *Scifaiku* seems to have become generally accepted among the writers concerned.

Steve Sneyd

[1] Harry Bose, **"Moons"**, *Star Line* March 1979
[2] Harry Bose, **"Second Thoughts"**, *Star Line* December 1979
[3] *Star Line* July 1981
[4] *Star Line* November 1982
[5] *Star Line* January 1983
[6] John Morris, **"How to Write Poems with a Computer"**, *Michigan Quarterly Review* 1967
[7] TABLE TALK 1827
[8] David Lunde, **"SF Haiku and Lyric Poetry"** *Star Line* March 1983
[9] http://www.scifaiku.com/index.html

RETURN TO HOME WORLD

full moon stays dead: beech
leaves howl same wind, bringing cold
scent of takeaways

MARS ARRIVAL

sight of so much red
maddens ...soon, metal horns point
straight down, rage to charge

Steve Sneyd

reddish orange glow
strange mist over blackened ground
metallic pterodactyls descend

walking starlit roads
ancient traveller stops the clocks
visit to small planet

Victoria Tarrani

This Autumn midnight
Orion's at my window
shouting for his dog.

Carol A. Coiffait

in the low
clouds Orion's feet
disappear

Jason Sanford Brown

under the covers
making elaborate plans
for the eclipse

Thom Williams

no other sound
the church bell rings out
through the Milky Way

Max Verhart

the flowers of Hell
bloom on Bikini Atoll
— nuclear winter

Jim Bennett

thunder frightens me
lightning sets fire to the sky
last drop overwhelms

Vaughn Banting

Wind-blown waves of grass
on the gently curving hill
lap dark standing stones

John Light

TANKA: WITH FEELING

Though less well known outside of Japan than its younger cousin, haiku, tanka have already appeared among the works of such major poets as Jorge Luis Borges and Caroline Kizer. The genre has been at the core of Japanese poetry for over a thousand years and involves millions of active poets in Japan today. And Japanese-style linked poetry seems to have evolved from the practice of two poets writing one tanka together.

Japan's most popular tanka poet today is Machi Tawara (b. 1963), whose first book sold well over three million copies in two years. The most readily available translations of her work into English are in three lines and do not reflect the structures of the originals.

Here is one of Tawara's poems, first as translated by Juliet Winters Carpenter, then phrase-by-phrase in romanized Japanese and in a quite literal version that illustrates the order of the phrases and approximates the duration of the original:

> I watch you on your surfboard
> poised between blueness
> of sky and sea [1]

sora no ao	the blue of the sky
umi no aosa no	and the blue hue of the sea–
sono awai	in that interval–
sâfubôdo no	at you on the surfboard
kimi o mitsumeru [2]	I stare intently [19]

The first of these may be engaging free verse in English, but it is not tanka. The Japanese is contemporary, but not casual. And the intensity of the space between the blues of sky and sea is paired with the intensity of the gaze connecting the observer and the object of observation, her lover; no mere watching, this.

Tanka originated as formal – and often playful – verses on love. Love of place, love of country, love of nature, and, most prominently, love and the loss of love between a man and a woman. In typical tanka, as in the example just given, a natural phenomenon, presented as itself, takes on a metaphorical value in the second part, where an emotional twist often floods back to color the whole poem. In the following tanka by a classical master, Lady Izumi (ca. 970-1030), the entire poem is metaphorical; the palpable images give that metaphor life:

kuraki yori	from the dark
kuraki michi ni zo	into a darker path
irinu beki	I must enter–
haruka ni terase	shine on in the distance
yama no ha no tsuki[3]	moon of the mountain ridge [19]

The moon here refers to the teaching of her spiritual mentor, Priest Shôku, to whom the poem was sent. The darkness indicates the student's difficulties, which can only be overcome by devoted adherence to the light of that teaching.

As these examples show, tanka, unlike haiku, often depend on metaphor for their meaning and power. Some, however, like the following by a modern poet who helped revolutionize the genre, Shiki Masaoka (1867-1902), are in fact very haiku-like and unmetaphorical:

matsu no ha no	each needle
ha goto ni musubu	of the needled pine holds
shiratsuyu no	the white dew
okite wa kobore	that forms and then scatters
koborete wa oku[4]	scatters and then forms [19]

For Japanese readers the poem may take on extra meaning from the traditional association of the pine with longevity and dew with transience, but this is *added* meaning, not *the* meaning. Shiki demanded the same kinds of clarity in tanka that he insisted on in haiku, for which he is better known in the West.

During its formative period before the Manyôshû (ca. 905 C.E.), a tanka consisted of two 12-sound units followed by a final unit in seven sounds, giving the poem a gentle feeling of closure. The 12-sound units break into five and seven sounds at the caesura, accounting for the usual description of the form as 31 sounds in a pattern of 5-7-5-7-7, though an excess of one or two sounds in a line may be allowed. Before the Shinkokinshû (ca. 1210), tanka poets began to capitalize on another natural break, the shift from the so-called "upper verse" (5-7-5) to the "lower verse" (7-7), producing a balance similar to that of the octave and the sestet in the Italian sonnet. This form continues in popularity today.

49

(Note: Older tanka are often called waka, a broader classification that includes the tanka of the courtly era. Westerners should be careful how they use the word "waka", however, since it literally and specifically means "poem(s) in Japanese language" [i.e., excluding even Chinese loanwords]. It is thus foolish to apply the word "waka" to modern Japanese poems that do not observe courtly diction, or to those written in languages other than Japanese.)

In the West, tanka have most often been presented as poems in five lines, one for each unit of the sound pattern in Japanese. Many academic translators, from Donald Keene onward, present translations in counted syllables in this pattern, which usually results in a poem overstuffed with both content and grammar, by Japanese standards. Some English-language poets use this form in their own original work. Such poems usually strike the ear as 50 to 100 percent longer than their Japanese counterparts, but may have merits of their own.

Formally, tanka in English have ranged from five short lines of free verse to 31 counted syllables. However, the form of 2-3-2-3-3 accented beats, as in the translations above, creates a recognizable English rhythm not otherwise present in our poetry, and has guided my own composition in the medium. Other translators who compose original work in English may also inform their practice with the modes they use in translation. For example, Sanford Goldstein, the premiere translator of modern Japanese tanka into English (see the bibliography), emulates his spare five-line, free-form translations in his own poems, often to telling effect.

But if tanka take up an important place in English-language poetry, it will be the work of other poets that makes it important. Wyatt was not Spenser, Sidney, or Shakespeare. Accordingly, the following tanka are by English-speaking poets who know little or no Japanese -- with the exception of Goldstein and Higginson. These poems do incorporate the typical themes and emotional range of Japanese tanka. The translated Japanese examples include works by prominent twentieth-century poets. The English originals span thirty years, in roughly the order of first publication; about half are within the last decade.

I should also mention that, just as haiku has its satiric senryu counterpart, there is a humorous tanka-manqué, called by the Japanese kyôka, or "mad poems"; the last two of the following group are interesting examples in English. For poems from the earlier courtly tradition, see the works mentioned in the bibliography.

Midway there
feelings changed suddenly,
I took a holiday from the office,
and today as well
cooled down by the river bank.

Takuboku Ishikawa (1886-1912) [19] *(The original counts 5-7-10-3-8)*

In the mouth
of a man cutting ice
I saw the red
glow of a cigarette
and kept on running.

Mokichi Saitô (1882-1953) [19]

Spring is short–
what lives to be immortal?
I thought
and let his hands seek
my powerful breasts.

Akiko Yosano (1878-1942) [19]

My husband and
child have long been in bed.
Why am I excited
under the midnight lamp?
I push the window open.

Miyoko Gotô (1898-1978) *translation by Reiko Tsukimura* [5]

In early dawn doze,
she comes to our bed and says,
the sun's coming up:
but when I reach to touch her,
she vanishes and I wake.

Carrow Devries [6]

on the wall
in a streak of sun
faded pencil lines–
my brother
he was that small

Michael McClintock [7]

want to walk
this spring day
and turn desire
on a spit
until it's done

Sanford Goldstein [8]

almost touch
a crumbling wall
stop
remembering
structure's fragility

Geraldine C. Little [9]

the cold walk,
silence
between us
the creek running
under ice

Tom Clausen [10]

the wind blown clouds
lighten and darken
lighten and darken
the room
in which we argue

Brian Tasker [11]

we even made love
under that ancient oak
one summer night–
it's gone to firewood
and now the firewood's gone

David C. Rice [12]

I walk by the park
where we first met–
its lamplights flicker
as the early morning rain
clings to the summer grass.

Annie Bachini [13]

my hands
just washed
yet i
wash them again
after the news

George Swede [14]

cutting potatoes
before she boils them
she finds herself
staring back at
all those eyes

Penny Harter [15]

a woman walks
ill-shod for the rough
beside the road
I'd offer her a ride
but for the consequences . . .

William J. Higginson [16]

Kyôka

>doing laundry
>after the argument—
>for a moment
>she holds his best shirt
>by the collar

Michael Dylan Welch [17]

>Mrs. Singleton
>has discovered herself
>She has freedom
>and quiet
>and alimony

Pat Shelley [18]

SELECTED BIBLIOGRAPHY

Akihito, Emperor, and Empress Michiko, *Tomoshibi: Light: Collected Poetry by Emperor Akihito and Empress Michiko*, edited by Marie Philomène and Masako Saito. Tokyo, Weatherhill, 1991. Altogether over 300 poems; a rich look at the persistence of the courtly tradition, this collection includes original Japanese texts and romanizations in an appendix; the translations are faithful.

Brower, Robert H., and Earl Miner, *Japanese Court Poetry*. Stanford University Press, 1961. The standard academic study on the subject. Good background; the translations are hardly poetry.

Chôbunsai, Eishi, editor and illustrator. *The Thirty-Six Immortal Women Poets (Nishikizuri onna sanjûrokkasen)*, introduction, commentaries, and translations by Andrew J. Pekarik. New York, George Braziller, 1991. Gorgeous ukiyoe prints with a poem or two by each poet, with excellent commentary. Pekarik gets my vote as the best translator of classical waka into 31 syllables in English.

Gotô, Miyoko, I Am Alive: *The Tanka Poems of Gotô Miyoko, 1898-1978*, translated by Reiko Tsukimura. Oakland, Katydid Books, 1988. I find her the most impressive modern tanka poet; she lived a long life and moved through many different phases, exploring each one to its end. The translations are among the best of all modern tanka. Includes original Japanese text.

Hirshfield, Jane, and Mariko Aratani, translators. *The Ink Dark Moon: Love Poems by Ono no Komachi and Izumi Shikibu, Women of the Ancient Court of Japan*. New York, Vintage Books, 1990. Excellent translations of these two richly rewarding poets. Japanese texts in romanization, good notes, and a fine introduction placing the poets in their milieux.

Ishikawa, Takuboku, *Romaji Diary and Sad Toys*, translated by Sanford Goldstein and Seishi Shinoda. Rutland, Charles E. Tuttle Co., 1985. The most comprehensive look at the writings of an early, influential modernist tanka poet. Fine translations, with originals and romanized Japanese.

Ishikawa Takuboku, *Takuboku: Poems to Eat*, translated by Carl Sesar. Tokyo. Kodansha International, 1966. Includes tanka not translated elsewhere, with Japanese texts. Still my favorite collection of Takuboku's work in English.

Lowitz, Leza, et al., editors and translators, *A Long Rainy Season: Haiku & Tanka*, Vol. I of Contemporary Japanese Women's Poetry. Berkeley, Stone Bridge Press, 1994. Includes varying numbers of tanka by eight contemporary Japanese poets, in free-form but relatively dependable five-line translations.

Masaoka, Shiki, *Songs from a Bamboo Village: Selected Tanka from Take no Sato Uta*, translated by Sanford Goldstein and Seishi Shinoda. Shiki, known in America mainly as the first great modern haiku poet, also revolutionized tanka and short prose essays. This collection gives the first fulsome look at his tanka in English. Introduction, translations, romanized Japanese text, and thorough notes.

Ôoka, Makoto, *A Poet's Anthology: The Range of Japanese Poetry*, translated by Janine Beichman. Santa Fe, Katydid Books, 1994. Comprehensive short overview of Japanese poetry, traditional and modern; extensive commentary by Japan's leading modern poet and one of her most popular critics. Excellent translations.

Reichhold, Jane, and Werner Reichhold, *Wind Five Folded: An Anthology of English-Language Tanka*. Gualala, Aha Books, 1994. A substantial collection that gives an overview of the range of activity in English.

Saigyô, *Songs of a Mountain Home*, translated by Burton Watson. New York, Columbia U P, 1990. Watson has brought more work from classical Japanese and Chinese into English than perhaps anyone and presents fine translations. Saigyô (1118-1190) was one of the greatest creators of the late court poetry.

Saitô, Mokichi, *Red Lights: Selected Tanka Sequences from Shakkô*, translated by Seishi Shinoda and Sanford Goldstein. West Lafayette, Purdue University Press, 1989. This team's usual fine translations and excellent introduction make this often intensely personal poetry accessible. Includes Japanese text and romanization.

Shôtetsu, *Unforgotten Dreams: Poems by the Zen Monk Shôtetsu*, translated by Steven D. Carter. New York, Columbia U P, 1997. Carter is one of the best academic translators of Japan's traditional poetry, and this book gives a deep view of the work of Shôtetsu (1381?-1459?), who lived during the ascendancy of the linked poem and still clung to the way of the uta that we know today as tanka. Includes romanized Japanese texts and introduction.

Tawara, Machi, *Salad Anniversary*, Jack Stamm, translator. Tokyo, Kawade Shobo Shinsha, 1988. A somewhat different selection from the Carpenter volume (see below), in much more faithful translations as to both form and content. Includes the Japanese text.

Tawara, Machi, *Salad Anniversary*, Juliet Winters Carpenter, translator. Tokyo, Kodansha International, 1989. Poorly done translations that often miss the spirit of the originals, as well as the form. (Un)fortunately, the Japanese originals are not included in any form.

Ueda, Makoto, *Modern Japanese Tanka: An Anthology*. New York, Columbia U P, 1996. The one book of its kind in English; excellent translations of a great range of work by twentieth-century Japanese poets. Not to be missed.

Welch, Michael Dylan, ed., *Footsteps in the Fog*. Foster City, Press Here, 1994. A fine, if slender, small press anthology of tanka by American poets writing in English.

Yosano, Akiko, *Tangled Hair: Selected Tanka from Midaregami*, Sanford Goldstein and Seishi Shinoda, translators. Lafayette, Purdue University Studies, 1971. Still my favorite presentation of Akiko in English, this beautifully designed book with fine translations, full Japanese texts and rômaji, deserves a reprint.

Yosano, Akiko, *River of Stars: Selected Poems*, translated by Sam Hamill and Keiko Matsui Gibson. Boston, Shambala, 1997. A broader range of fewer poems, with a number of her longer poems as well as tanka. Reasonable translations, no Japanese except for the occasional kanji in fine calligraphy by Stephen Addiss.

William J. Higginson

[1] *Salad Anniversary*, Kodansha International, p9. © Kodansha International, 1989, by permission of the publisher.

[2] *Sarada Kinenbi*, Kawade Shobo Shinsha, 1987.

[3] Shûishû (c.1000), #1342.

[4] source for the original: Janine Beichman, Masaoka Shiki, Twayne, 1982, p93.

[5] *I Am Alive*, Katydid Books, 1988, p66. © Reiko Tsukimura, 1988, by permission of the publisher.

[6] *Moment of Flower and Leaf*, privately printed.

[7] *Thief: Diary Notes*, privately printed, 1972. By permission of the author.

[8] *This Tanka World* Purdue Poets Coop, 1977, p26. © Sanford Goldstein, 1977, by permission of the author.

[9] *The Spinalonga Poems*, Wind Chimes, 1986. © Geraldine C. Little, 1986 by permission of the publisher.

[10] *Tanka Splendor 1992*, AHA Books, 1992, p14. © AHA Books, 1993, by permission of the author.

[11] *Blithe Spirit*, 4:1 (Feb 1994), p23. By permission of the author.

[12] *Footsteps in the Fog*, Press Here, 1994, p14. © Michael D. Welch, 1994, by permission of the publisher.

[13] *Blithe Spirit*, 5:1 (Feb 1995), p24. By permission of the author.

[14] *Humingbird* V:2 (Dec 1994), p31. © Phyllis Walsh, 1994, by permission of the author.

[15] © Penny Harter, 2000

[16] *Five Lines Down* #1 (Summer 1994), p14. © Five Lines Down, 1994, by permission of the author.

[17] *Tanka Splendor 1993*, AHA Books, 1993. © AHA Books, 1994, by permission of the author.

[18] *Footsteps in the Fog*, Press Here, 1994 p22. © Michael D. Welch, 1994, by permission of the publisher.

[19] These translations were prepared for this article by William J. Higginson, © William J. Higginson, 2000, by permission of the translator.

i waited all year for the
first spring blossoms to appear
and yet, i long for endless
winter nights counting
amber stars with you

Pamela A. Babusci

Naked children crowd
as I pass through the alleys
between smelly slums:
dogs bark to alert them to
the presence of a stranger

R. K. Singh

wind and ocean rise
capture my tears as they fall
...the night cries
of a thousand plovers
cannot cover my own

newborn
screaming, screaming
all through the night
incessant memories
of her conception

Linda Jeannette Ward

river rain
re-telling
your daughter
your stories
in my voice

no one
to sip tea with
still i warm
a second
teabowl

ai li

no stars last night
and this morning the cliff's edge
has disappeared
    I think a dog is barking
    and the clock is ticking
          sometimes
          she sent me to the store
          and sometimes
               I bought baby peas
               instead of carrots

Leatrice Lifshitz

It is like a scream
    this powerful April gale
        of too many amps
    you could shriek an opera
or play a *Merman* record
        what can you do when
            vet diagnosis crop's ripped
             maybe broken wing
             stench of death from its torn flesh
        still it says I want to live?

Joan Payne Kincaid

really   fire
feels   aurora's
minimal —   beneath
the   far
cancer   freezing
to
my
tongue   **John Ower**

ON THE ROAD WITH HAIBUN

As with any complicated art form, haibun is difficult to define to anyone's satisfaction. But briefly, and far-too-simplified, haibun is a combination of at least two, and sometimes three elements, each a demanding art in itself: vivid descriptive prose, haiku, and sometimes haiga (the elegant impressionistic paintings that often accompany both haibun and haiku).

Despite the appearance of simplicity, haibun is a complex and rigorous art. Some call haibun travel journals or diaries. However, these classifications can cause misunderstandings since such descriptions capture only a part of what haibun is. It is actually much more than that. Primarily it is a literary production, and as with any other literary creation it strives to be interesting, informative, and inventive. It is not private writing, like some journals and diaries, but is meant for the eyes of readers. Literary haibun strives to share a story, an experience, an insight, a journey of whatever kind as it attempts to touch readers emotionally, sensually, intellectually, and spiritually. While quite fluid, it is also based on certain solid principles.

As a disciple said about Matsuo Basho's writing theory, "one can learn about pine only from the pine, about bamboo only from the bamboo..." [1] The same idea can extend to learning about haibun: one can learn about haibun only from haibun. A brief and general look at the work of three important masters serves as a good starting point. The selections chosen for this anthology will help to understand more.

Matsuo Basho (1644-1694) is not only given credit for elevating haiku to an art form, but he is also credited with creating one of the most famous works of haibun in his *Oku-no-Hosomichi*. The title is referred to in various ways: *Narrow Path, Narrow Road, Narrow Road to a Far Province*, and more, and is significant to the contents of the haibun. Dorothy Britton claims the title is a tour de force, rich and dense with meaning, and believes Basho was suggesting a "peregrination into the inner reaches of the mind." Further, Britton thinks Basho chose this ambiguous and rich title in order "to embrace all its wider meanings" [2].

Oku-no-Hosomichi is one of the great works of Japanese literature, and Harold G. Henderson says it "has probably been annotated and commented on more than any other work of its size in the world" [3]. As testament to its importance, Yosa Buson (1716-83), another master of haiku and haibun, is said to have copied and illustrated this work at least ten times himself [4]. In an apt description, Soryo, the scholar priest who prepared the work for publication says Basho's "multifarious...limned impressions" create prose "as beautiful as mermaid's tears" [5].

Part of its greatness, says Hiroaki Sato, "lies in its doing so much with so little. Like a haiku it gets its vivid immediacy and sensory power from the suggestiveness created by its terse, laconic style. It is all at once a travel journal (kikibun), a haibun, a renga, and a haiku anthology." Basho shaped it this way deliberately, "changing the order and some of the events and even inventing some — to make it a work of art." Further, he asserts that "one could even describe this haibun as a series of about fifty short haibun which work with each other much like the links in a renga" [6]

Basho was influenced by a long tradition of wandering poets and was especially interested in the classical Chinese poets Li Po and Tu Fu, and in the classical Japanese poets Sogi, and Saigyo. It was customary for "literary and artistic notables or would-be notables" to make poetic pilgrimages and to publish their journals [7]. Basho, along with his disciples, set out on his own poetic pilgrimages and attempted to retrace some of the footsteps of poets who came before. In so doing he positioned himself in history, custom, and in a strong poetic tradition. The resulting haibun yields philosophical and religious thoughts, quotes from classical poetry, original and collaborative poetry, learned allusions, vignettes, myth and legend, landscapes, images, traces of history, glimpses of nature, and the effect all of it had on his own receptive mind.

Chiyo-ni (1703-1775), a Buddhist nun and haijin (haiku master) who also had a widely-acclaimed talent for painting haiga, followed the high standards set by Basho in her own poetic work. Like Basho she espoused haiku as a life's path and believed that the way of poetry was also the "way of refinement in one's life and art." For Chiyo-ni, poetry would be a source of awakening, and like Basho she was able to travel and write haiku on the road. She very likely wrote many haibun, as would have been customary, but unfortunately only one slim haibun remains: *Yoshizake Mode (Pilgrimage to Yoshizake)*. The haibun is dated 1762, when at sixty years old she fulfilled her dream of making this journey [8]. Because of its brevity, it is difficult to compare her work to Basho's. But Chiyo-ni was one of the greatest women poets of the Edo period and her extant haibun, short as it is, contains poignant haiku, stirring images, wordplay, interesting and touching observations, and luminous comparisons.

Another haijin was Kobayashi Issa (1763-1827) whose most renowned piece is *Oraga-Haru*. The title literally means *"My Spring"* but is often translated as *The Year of My Life* because ostensibly it traces out the cycle of a year, beginning in the spring with the Japanese New Year. However, the year Issa writes about was not a literal year, but "is inspired and shaped by all of a fully lived life" [9]. Lewis Mackenzie says the serene-toned haiku within "have a kind of evening glow on them not of this world" [10]. His works, says Sam Hamill, "reveal a deep engagement with the teachings of Zen, as well as with the Way of Haiku advocated by Basho, and it is probably for these strengths of character, including his unabashed honesty, that he was admired by almost everyone regardless of social rank" [11] Issa's haibun is extraordinarily touching, revealing an all-too-human journey filled with poverty, devastating losses, doubts, and yearnings. His work reveals a startling clarity of vision, profound insights, and is full of myth and legend, quotes, irony, paradox, humor, and tragedy. *Oraga-Haru* is excruciatingly beautiful.

Reading the haibun of Basho, Chiyo-ni, and Issa gives a good beginning grounding in this type of writing. These three masters helped set the standards for those who came later, and haibun has continued to grow in writer and reader interest. It has also taken strong root in North America, mainly through those who formed the Beat Movement of the 1950s. According to Bruce Ross, Gary Snyder's *Earth House Hold* (1957) "approaches haibun in tone and structure" and he says that Snyder's *Lookout's Journal* "offers a model of what American haibun was to become" [12]. Jack Kerouac, in collaboration with Albert Saijo and Lew Welch, wrote another book-length haibun called *Trip Trap: Haiku on the Road* which records their road trip from San Francisco to New York in 1959. However, it wasn't published until 1973, and then a revised edition was published in 1998. The haibun contains vivid and sometimes surprising prose, prose poetry, haiku, and even some rather crude haiga [13].

However, haibun is not limited to book-length work. It can be as short as a prose paragraph that ends with a haiku, it can begin with a haiku, it can have haiku within paragraphs, and, as Cor van den Heuvel points out, it can even be haiku-prose with no haiku [14]. Much of the charm of haibun derives from the way it occupies several thresholds: prose, poetry, prose poetry, journal and diary writing, autobiography, travel and nature writing, non-fiction and even fiction — for who can tell when non-fiction and fiction actually part company? In fact, both Basho and Issa in part "fictionalized" their haibun to help it conform to important aesthetic literary balances [15]. Further, in recent times what is called *American haibun* also shows a strong kinship with certain other short-short pieces such as flash, micro, and sudden fiction [16]. Haibun is flexible, versatile, protean — can assume many forms and shapes. It is conducive to experimentation and innovation.

Whether short or book-length, it remains a demanding art. According to Elizabeth St Jacques, the characteristics of quality haibun include: —

work written in present tense — haibun works best when the reader receives a sense of "nowness,"

the writing must be focused (clear and to the point) and simply stated (free from intellectualizing, flowery or "cute" wording),

written about a subject that moves readers (but without being saccharine, overly sentimental, or in bad taste),

written with a touch of humor to give the reader some reprieve and to emphasize the reality of life itself,

the accompanying haiku must not repeat from the text but must provide something fresh, unexpected (many new writers of haibun make the mistake of telling too much before presenting a haiku and/or the haiku repeats),

has a title that captures the attention but doesn't repeat from the text or telegraph what to expect (new writers can't be reminded of this too often) [17].

According to Michael D. Welch, haibun "is a broadening of haiku to embrace many–but not all–prose possibilities, yet correctly aligning the two mirrors of prose and poetry to seek the perfect amalgamation of haibun is fraught with subjective aesthetic challenges" [18]. George Swede adds, "most haibun fail because they do not effectively integrate the prose with the haiku. In most cases, the relationship is strained, i.e., not like the embrace between the two in Basho's *Narrow Road to a Far Province*" [19]. Rod Willmot, who wrote *The Ribs of the Dragonfly* (1984), a sensuous haibun novella, says he sees some common failings in some published haibun: "first, when short snippets of prose are interspersed with scatterings of haiku, the two blend together and the reader reads too quickly; second, too often the prose sets up the haiku so plainly that there is no surprise" [20].

Despite the demands of the art of haibun, there are many quality writers publishing their fine work in several outstanding North American journals and anthologies (*Modern Haiku, Frogpond, Cicada, Snow on the Water* to name just a few). Several recent chapbooks have been published as well and the haibun ranges from more traditional haibun to the highly experimental and innovative American haibun of Sheila Murphy [21]. Several recent high quality anthologies have appeared on the scene and others are planned. The Internet too is playing a large part in spreading interest in haibun with more and more sites featuring haiku, haibun, traditional haiga and even computer-graphics haiga.

As Basho said in his *Oku-no-Hosomichi*, in an allusion to the work of Li Po, "The months and days are wayfarers of a hundred generations, and the years that come and go are also travelers" [22]. In our travels, whether literally to far-off lands or in our travel through our days and lives, we encounter our worlds and we encounter ourselves. Literary haibun can teach us much about the amazing journeys we all share.

Pamelyn Casto

[1] Patricia Donegan and Yoshie Ishibashi, Chiyo-ni: Woman Haiku Master 1998.

[2] Dorothy Britton, A Haiku Journey: Basho's Narrow Road to a Far Province 1974.

[3] Harold G. Henderson, An Introduction to Haiku 1958.

[4] Hiroaki Sato, Basho's Narrow Road: Spring & Autumn Passages 1996.

[5] Britton 1974.

[6] Sato 1996.

[7] Lewis Mackenzie, The Autumn Wind: A Selection from the Poems of Issa 1984.

[8] Donegan and Ishibashi 1998.

[9] Sam Hamill, The Spring of My Life and Selected Haiku by Kobayashi Issa 1997.

[10] Mackenzie 1984.

[11] Hamill 1997.

[12] Bruce Ross, Journey to the Interior: American Versions of Haibun 1998.

[13] Jack Kerouac, Albert Saijo, Lew Welch, Trip Trap: Haiku on the Road 1998.

[14] Cor van den Heuvel, "Foreword", Sato 1996.

[15] Sato, 1998 and Hamill 1997.

[16] Stewart Dybek, "Toward A New Form", Sudden Fiction: American Short-Short Stories, Robert Shapard and James Thomas, eds. 1986.

[17] Elizabeth St Jacques, email letter to the author, 28 August 1999.

[18] Michael D. Welch, Wedge of Light 1999.

[19] George Swede, email letter to the author, 28 August 1999.

[20] Rodd Willmot, email letter to the author, 31 August 1999.

[21] Sheila Murphy, Mudlark 1998
        http://www.unf.edu/mudlark/mudlark08/contents.html

[22] Sato 1996.

A MOTH FOR LA TOUR

On the cover of *Smithsonian* there's a painting of a gypsy girl by Georges de La Tour, a close-up shot revealing tiny cracks in the aged canvas; yet this renaissance maid appears young and fresh: her round face framed by a kerchief folded tight to her head and tied in a simple little knot under her chin, no hint of hair exposed, no wispy stray escaping. Shades of copper and rose blend together across finely cracked cheeks, her eyes portrayed in a sideways glance, engaged in trickery, the text says.

On the table beside me this magazine has mysteriously attracted a moth whose copper and rose wings perfectly match the gypsy's cheek where it rests almost camouflaged, as if the artist, weary of painting only people, had endeavored to add a touch of nature for a more rustic look.

I don't know how this tiny moth found its way inside and what instinct urged it to a surface so foreign to its natural home, yet so like its own softly colored wings. I want to leave it there, a reminder of how magic life can be.

barely visible
on her painted cheek
rose and copper moth

Linda Jeannette Ward

THE UNEVEN PATH

In the Japanese Tea Garden, I stand facing the bronze statue of Buddha. There is no disturbance of voices, the nearby tea house being empty of tourists, and the paths all but deserted due to a thunderstorm. The smooth gray flagstones are glossed with rain, and the only sound is a gentle drumming on the tan silk umbrella . . . A plum petal drifts down and sticks to the umbrella, pressed into focus by the weight of raindrops. A second petal falls, and settles in the Buddha's left hand, the one resting palm up on his lap.

In another direction the trunk of a gnarled black pine slowly darkens. As I watch, I remember a favorite story about a certain monk. I'm not sure when the incident was to have taken place, if indeed it did, but the truth of the message makes the factuality of the account superfluous.

A young monk was sitting stiffly in front of a likeness of the Buddha. He'd been there for most of the day when the temple's abbot happened to pass by and noticed the devout intensity of the monk's zazen. So he approached, and stood beside the monk for a while, gazing at the bronze figure. All at once, the abbot hawked up a huge wad of phlegm and spat onto the statue's face. There was silence for a long moment while the incredulous monk regained his composure. "Sacrilege!" he at last gasped, and demanded his teacher explain why he'd done such an unthinkable thing. Of course, the answer came immediately: "Where can you spit, and not hit Buddha?"

I admire the pine for a while, then move on. The rain has stopped and, as I wander back along the uneven path of puddles, amid flurries of drifting petals, I can feel the Buddha's eyes on my back.

narrow stepping stone
a short wait
for the snail to cross

Christopher Herold

QUASHING

Rendering *just this* a lean while, often supposing memoranda chafe sequential liens during the keepsake hours of need. The voids in our community remand clichés and steel themselves clean of prior whittles. Jam-packed for the sake of hyping crates of energy called *source* and seepage herein with a causeway blinking and a sequined roster where the mainframe can be costed out for worthiness. These framed wood elements. These cleave canaries. This embossed blue fitting wood. Why not importune the glistening ivy. The gemlike roster. And the seventeen careers. The moment loss comes by, out comes the soap. People distancing in case of failure. In case of posted wall space. In case of fill dirt. Deemed a pistol, deemed a race, deemed pituitary. Here within the game we're rolling sharp dice outside all smooth crevicings. To blanche the night away in time for waltzed incendiary pliés tipped to mean your uncle's wide, meandering across fallopia.

Gym clothes, false wheat, water hose, all this myopia

Sheila E. Murphy

65

SYLLABIC POETRY:
REVIVAL OF THE SEDOKA VIA THE SIJO?

Iambic verse is a predominating form of verse in many languages, and in traditional English poetry, the iambic pentameter has always been the most common metre. It was used by Pope, Dryden and of course, Shakespeare. There is a similar situation in Japanese poetry, where the attention to sound leads to the English language equivalent of either a five-syllable line, a seven-syllable line, or various combinations of both. The most common example of this usage appears in the formal haiku.

Haiku and tanka are now established poetic forms in several European languages. *Waka* is a general term of all Japanese poems employing a fixed form and refers to *yamatouta (Japanese poem)* as opposed to *karauta (Chinese poem)*. It includes the *katauta* which, like haiku employs the 5-7-5 pattern. Literally katauta means *"part of a poem"*, because this verse is not meant to stand alone. The longer form, *choka* employs alternating lines of 5 and 7 syllables, concluding with a 7-syllable line. A tanka could be considered a short *choka*. Another older related form is the *sedoka*. This consists of 38 syllables arranged in six lines, 5-7-7-5-7-7. The name means *"head-repeated-poem"*. The form was rarely used after the early period of Japanese Literature (782-1155).

That Spring night I spent	Falling from the ridge
Pillowed on your arm	Of a high Tsukuba
Never really happened	The Minano River
Except in a dream	At last gathers itself,
Unfortunately I am	Like my love, into
Talked about anyway	A deep, still pool.
Lady Suo (11th cent.)	**The Emperor Yozei** (877-884) [1]

Perhaps the sedoka will be unwittingly resurrected on the back of the *sijo*, the most typical form of Korean lyrics, *sijo* means *"melody of time"*. It was originally a very rigid form written in three lines and content-wise, closely related to nature and the geographic situation. The sijo derives from the old Hyangka Songs of the Sylla Empire (668-936) and the prose songs of the Koryo Kingdom (918-1392). There are three forms: *chung sijo* and *chang sijo* have greater syllable counts and irregular line lengths, while *pyongsijo* is the form adopted by Western writers.

GOING

a fiddle in the distance
the traveller closes the door
inside the silence grows

HVIIDS VINSTUE [1]

a clear
glass
of wine

on a dark
well worn
table

someone
will be
back -

Árni Ibsen

translated from Icelandic by Árni Ibsen and Petur Knutsson

---

[1] *Hviids Vinstue* (literally "White's Wine Parlour") is the name of a very old and famous pub cum restaurant in the centre of Copenhagen, Denmark. It was the traditional hang-out of numerous Icelandic intellectuals while studying in the capital, especially the beloved 19th century romantic poet Jónas Hallgrímsson (1807-1845).

HAIKU AND SCIENCE EDUCATION

Nature lies at the heart of science. Scientists attempt to explain nature's patterns and details. Haiku, too, is a study of nature. Poets capture their experience of the world around them in words. Thus, while haiku and science instruction may seem to some like a strange coupling, this article describes the benefits of integrating haiku writing with the teaching of science. By helping students become more aware of their surroundings, writing haiku encourages curiosity about the natural phenomena taught in science courses and fosters several fundamental scientific skills

We have taught students of diverse ages to write haiku as part of their curriculum. While we discuss the traditional syllabic pattern of haiku, our primary emphasis is on succinctly and powerfully capturing observations of nature with words. Initially students are taken to natural areas during class, but as the term progresses, they are encouraged to capture moments with nature wherever and whenever they occur. In other words, students are encouraged to notice the extraordinary in the ordinary These examples of student work are shown below with their permission:

> Roses are blooming.
> The dew is starting to drip
> as the sun rises.
> **Kayla Cummings** (age 9)

> In winter stillness
> Icy breezes softly flow.
> Suddenly wind BLOWS.
> **Arlene Diaz** (age 12)

> Cicada buzzing
> Grasping the old knotted tree
> Sun burning his back
> **Christopher Spire** (adult student)

> Angled wings, tail spread
> The hawk rides an air current
> Into the distance
> **Natalie Lewis** (adult student)

Teaching students to write haiku in this way helps them develop a number of skills important to scientific literacy.

Observational skills

Observation is central to the nature of science. Questions investigated by scientists are based on observations, and these observations are used to evaluate the validity of hypotheses.

Writing haiku requires students to observe nature. While children are naturally curious about the world around them, many have never been taught to quietly observe the outside world without disruption. As children mature into adults, many become too busy and hurried to notice nature's subtle details. Haiku writing fosters skills needed to become better observers. It thereby engages students in this fundamental process of science.

Distinguishing between observation and inference

Data gathered using the five senses are observations. Scientists infer explanations for observed phenomena and then evaluate their validity with experimentation and further observations. Science students, however, often confuse inference and observation since inferences frequently seem so obvious or intuitive from a human perspective. The frenzied activity of ants around an anthill may be interpreted as excitement, a singing bird may be inferred to be joyful or a wilting plant sad. It is important for students to recognize that these are only possible explanations for these behaviors. Haiku includes only descriptions of observations, leaving the interpretation of these captured experiences to the individual reader. Thus, learning to write haiku gives students practice distinguishing between observation and inference. Clarifying the distinction improves the quality of their haiku and their scientific reasoning.

Communication Skills

Science, like haiku, values clear, concise communication. Scientists must record their observations accurately, logically, and completely. Writing haiku encourages the development of two critical writing skills: precise selection of words and sequencing of ideas towards a powerful conclusion.

Experience with Nature

In our increasingly technological and urbanized society, many children grow up with reduced contact with the natural world. Thus, it is incumbent upon parents and teachers to create opportunities for children to gain more firsthand experiences with natural phenomena. Cultivating opportunities for students to write haiku places them in contact with the outside world. Personal experience with nature helps develop respect, appreciation, and a sense of wonder–attributes that are critical for the future custodians of planet Earth. It also fosters curiosity and positive attitudes toward learning science.

The process of science, of course, goes beyond observing and recording. While haiku focuses on observation, the experiences with nature captured in haiku can become "jumping off points" to meet additional science education goals, such as being able to ask questions or construct a reasonable explanation for a phenomenon. A logical follow-up to the writing of haiku is to ask what questions the students have about what they observed and what ideas they have about the answers. This approach can generate a student-centered curriculum, in which scientific investigation focuses on topics of interest to the students. As one nine-year old said, "It [writing haiku] is fun. It's cool. I like doing it.... It is fun stuff because you learn more about the stuff you do it on.... Once you choose what you want to do it on you can go to a big...dictionary and you could read more about it and learn more."

Haiku invites students into nature. Time spent with nature invites students into science. And science educators can ask for nothing better than engaged audiences eager to learn more about the phenomena of nature. Writing haiku nurtures this inquisitiveness along with a number of requisite skills for scientific literacy.

Karen A. Conzelman, Peter Rillero and Jo Cleland

LEAP AND STAMP

The *"kasen"* is a popular traditional form of Japanese renku linked haikai consisting of a sequence of 36 verses. In medieval renga, solo *"dogkugin"* sequences were fairly common and became even more popular in haikai in the 17th century. In renga and haikai, alternating verses of three and two 'lines' or units of 5-7-5 and 7-7 syllables are used, but Japanese is an agglutinative language with numerous codes of implicit reference and without subject and other markers required by English, and I find that four- and three-line verses more closely approximate in English the expressive power of the compressed Japanese verses. Adjoining verses form one 'link'; the two-verse link moves as the reader moves onward. However, since the 17th century, a certain amount of wider connotative continuity beyond two adjacent verses can sometimes be found, and conceptual, dialogical, and psychological links have also been acceptable.

Students leap and stamp
down the front steps
of the old building
after the entrance exam

Balancing on the edge
of a garbage can, crows
explicate human history

Straw bags in hand,
farmers cross a field
looking for stones
and airplane bolts

"Right after the war they plowed
the lawn of the National Diet
and grew vegetables on it."

The prime minister
gazes outside
and thinks
of golf

In the next seat
the president of Mitsubishi Trading
points down at the Mekong

The diviner
holds up her twig,
spins another roll
of toilet paper

"Avoid men who speak
of absolute beauty and bodies
of water without heads."

Heron tracks
out on
the sandbar,
none on the shore

In two facing lines
women and men exchange songs,
choosing partners

Out in the dark,
sounds of shamisens
and legs
in the long grass

U.S. Marines
walk a narrow path
between paddies

Sleepless,
she stops again,
asks if anyone's seen
her missing daughter

"I'll call you
when I get my own number
here in Tokyo."

A flock of sparrows
smokes up from the wire
as the sun moves
behind Mt. Fuji

He switches on
the lamp, goes back
to his bonsai tree

Hotsprings room
clean, he waits for
a new busload of women
who'll choose him this time?

"I like your accent.
Much softer than the dirt
my husband speaks."

The gaze from the statue
of the smiling Buddha
passes out the door
toward the Pacific

The blind female shaman
feels the stone forehead, fingers
the socket of its third eye

To sax and drums
poet Shiraishi Kazuko routes
sensual subways, collects her city
in the underground accidents of her voice

The mayor turns down
the mike to reply to
angry council members

Dirty snow hits
the face of a policeman
advancing on a series
of cardboard houses

Cat blood or human,
frozen to the sidewalk
full moon in January

A young college president
meets student demands,
dies of heart failure
during a faculty meeting

Clouds of yellow dust,
birds flying backwards
in spring wind

Mountains flap
like last week's newspapers,
the capital lies whistling
around the hole of the present

She cuts out ads
for English-study videos
and four-night tours

Speaking wide phrases
on a wide bed
in the Sheraton Plaza
on Manhattan

The bell rings
for lunch in the office
of the industrial plant

Two months
behind on delivery
of homemade F-16s
to the Self Defense Forces

The widow
of the air-show pilot
opens an official envelope

Four old Korean women,
once sex slaves, sit with signs
and refuse to move
from the imperial palace gate

In the moat
carp huddle, catfish
tilt their whiskers

Teacups tinkle,
the bay shudders,
small things fall,
the stock market falls.

At the end of the aisle
a package of dried seaweed
still on the shelf

Chris Drake

TIPURITURA: A KIND OF ROMANIAN HAIKU

The *tipuritura* (phon. *tzipuritura*) is the shortest Romanian poetic form. Founded in the northern region of Maramures (phon. *Maramouresh*), it usually includes two lines with seven or eight syllables, but can have three or four lines, and is shouted to music at popular parties. Its main features are black humour and subtlety. The rhyme is obligatory

Normal Tipuritura

> Large place is Maramuresu,
> But hasn't fools like me and you.[1]

Cosmic Tipuritura

> I like a frisky girl, Sir,
> The Sun and Moon to beat her![1]

Long Tipuritura (could be considered the Romanian equivalent to the tanka, quatrain or limerick)

> "Make me, God, a nice rainbow
> To surround a belt of girl,
> And to climb faster to You!"
> "Perhaps to the Devil too!"[2]

Astro-Tipuritura[3]

> Hidden on an asteroid
> I thought: "The Sun is too timid."

> Comet with a tender face,
> Don't kiss the planets through space!
> **Andrei Dorian Gheorghe**

> Oh, I would climb up to the sky
> For the Pleiades' sons which fly

> Cassiopeia, shut up you,
> And give me your "double u".
> **Dan Mitrut**

Who are you, great Galaxy?
Only God could know and see...

This is the best world, but bad
When meteors scalp your head.
                    Dominic Diamant

Arrest that falling star, that light,
Not to burn the Earth on its flight.

Starry dust, cobweb, night rider,
I don't see your cosmic spider.
                    Victor Chifelea

Andrei Dorian Gheorghe

[1] Collected by Ion Bârlea.
[2] Collected by Ioan Slavici.
[3] composed by members of SARM (*Societatea Astronomică Română de Meteori*);
    English versions by Andrei Dorian Gheorghe.

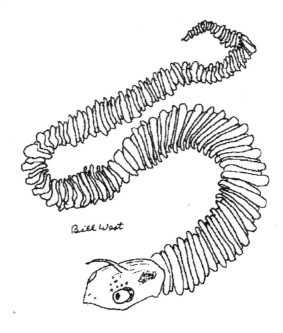

Bill West

POSITIVELY POETRY
An International Anthology of Little Press Poets, 1970-1995
Over 100 poets including Stella Browning, David Cobb, R.L. Cook, Mabel Ferrett, Eddie Flintoff, John Gonzalez, Roger Harvey, Brian Merrikin Hill, David Jaffin, Peter Thabit Jones, Anne Lewis-Smith, Nigel McLoughlin, Christopher Pilling, Andrea Sherwood, Steve Sneyd, Kenneth C. Steven, John Ward, Maureen Weldon and Leo Yankevich. **Artwork** by Cato, Ian M. Emberson, John Light, Joyce Mills, Ian Robinson, Geoff Stevens and Carmen Willcox
ISBN 0 903610 16 7 -   *£5.95*   *[£10 ex-UK]*

JOHN ELSBERG: SAILOR.
"In poems ranging formally from gentle rhythmic prolixity to near-concrete minimalism, Elsberg explores his relationship with his father ...the restraint and careful craftsmanship heighten the emotional impact by almost denying it."   *— Coal City Review*
ISBN 0 903610 23 X   *£3.75*   *[£5 ex-UK]*

GERALD ENGLAND: EDITOR'S DILEMMA
An account of 20 years of Small Press Publishing, including original poetry by George Cairncross, Cal Clothier, Andy Darlington, John Elsberg, Peter Finch, Geoffrey Holloway, Henny Kleiner, Anne Lewis-Smith, William Oxley, Margaret Perkins, Irene Twite &c.
ISBN 0 903610 10 8   *£1.50*   *[£2 ex-UK]*

B.Z.NIDITCH: ON THE EVE
"A summing up of a poetic career that scans decades and continents. The first poems are timeless stories, school days and birthdays. Further on, the enchor of history appears, with reflections on many events in Eastern Europe — Auschwitz, German culture, Stalin's death and Pasternak's. Dense with thickets of meaning, these are not poems to be casually scanned, but to be savoured and appreciated."
                                        — Factsheet Five.
ISBN 0 903610 07 8   *£1.50*   *[£2 ex-UK]*

ALBERT RUSSO: PAINTING THE TOWER OF BABEL

"Truly an internationalist by background the poems selected for this pleasing and impressive collection seem to build into a wide-screen overview of the world. Russo is not tied to any one corner and lets all his experiences enter the arena. Albert Russo is an accomplished and talented user of words."   — *Target.*

"At his best when trying to puzzle out the nature of reality ... features the poet's own photographs."   — *Zene.*

ISBN 0 903610 18 3   £3   *[£4 ex-UK]*

BRIGGFLATTS VISITED: A TRIBUTE TO BASIL BUNTING

Poems by Stella Browning, Gerald England, Sally Evans, Mabel Ferrett, Eleanor Makepeace, Malcolm Payne, Christopher Pilling, Colin Simms, John Ward; Articles by Chris Challis, Mabel Ferrett, Brian Merrikin Hill, William Oxley, Richard Livermore.

2nd edn. with new illustrations.

ISBN 0 903610 17 5   £3   *[£4 ex-UK]*

BRIAN BLACKWELL: THE SMILE OF LIES

In the Land of Birches, the poems which make up the second half of this collection, draw on the poet's experiences in Belarus, where he was a visiting lecturer. "he deftly counterpoints the observed world with the suffering that lies just below its surface....sharp and observant"

— *Target*

ISBN 0 903610 19 1   £3   *[£4 ex-UK}*

GILLIAN BENCE-JONES: OSTRICH CREEK

"What I like about *Ostrich Creek* is the ease with which Gillian Bence-Jones stimulates the ordinary. Waffle-free, the poems speak volumes in a rich swell of implicitness 'Twilight', 'The First', 'Safe as Houses', 'Sea-Beast' all bask in suppleness. I also enjoyed being taken on a trip abroad, skimming the surface of a new exotic culture ... the poems shift sand, are warmed and cooled by the tide of wonderful language"   — *The Affectionate Punch*

ISBN 0 903610 22 1   £6.95   *[£10 ex-UK]*

NOVIN AFROUZ: HOPE OF PEACE

First collection by the celebrated Iranian concert pianist and winner of *The Milan Peace Prize*. "Stirred by the dawn, the sea, flowers, the Revolution, wind, the poet vibrates, is deeply moved, sings, retying in the poem the sacred bonds of music and language."

—*Leopold Sadar Senghor*   (ex-President of Senegal).

ISBN 0 903610 04 3   £1.95   [£3 ex-UK]

JOHN MARKS: LIFTING THE VEIL

"refreshing both in the simplicity of form and in the way the poet uses words — his own and those given to others — unfussed, clear and immediate to the reader.... In all these poems the poet is visible, which also makes him vulnerable"   — *Iota*

ISBN 0 903610 20 5   £3.50   [£5 ex-UK]

GERALD ENGLAND: LIMBO TIME

"The range is impressive: haiku, tanka, sijo, sonnets, a semi-concrete sequence of *'squares'*. Whole landscapes and ways of life can be summed up in a few lines... this is a kind of selected Gerald England, and new readers could well start here."   — *Zene*

"Gerald England shows his ability to make imagery work to create the atmosphere, resonance and feeling and mastery of apt and original language."   — *Weyfarers*

ISBN 0 903610 21 3   £3.75   [£5 ex-UK]

"NINETY NINETY"

A 90-min tape of poetry, music & fun featuring Chris Challis, Dave Cunliffe, Andy Darlington, Eddie Flintoff, Tom Grierson, Roger Harvey, Peter Thabit Jones, Lord Litter, Gwen Wade, John Ward, Glenda Wintein & more.   £3   [£5 ex-UK]

More information on these and other publications available can be found on the NHI Website at

http://www.nhi.clara.net/nhibooks.htm